THE AVERAGE MUSIC LOVER'S GUIDE TO
SERIOUS MUSIC OF THE 20th CENTURY

HOW TO LISTEN TO MODERN MUSIC WITHOUT EARPLUGS

DAVID E. WALDEN

Sound And Vision

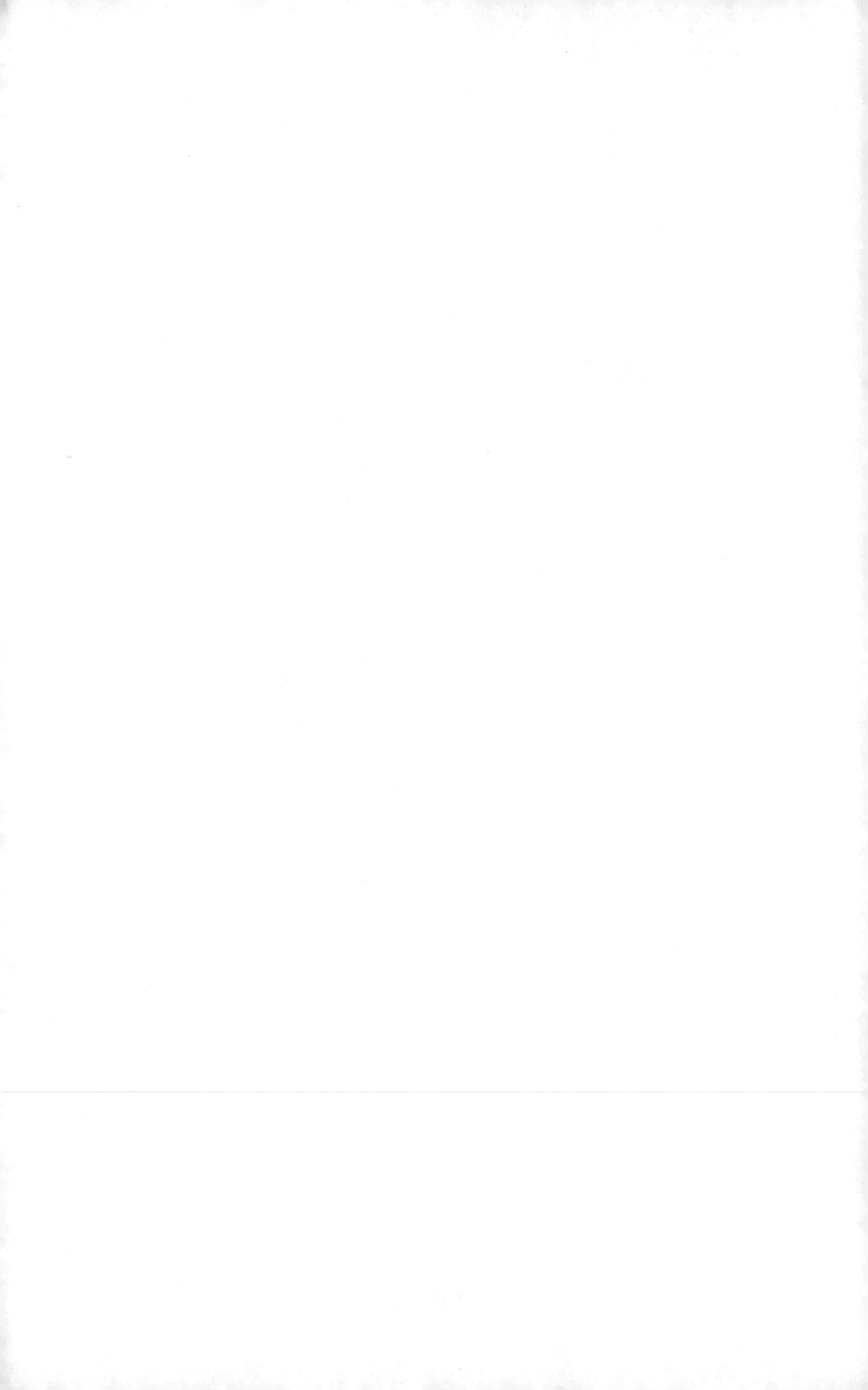

THE AVERAGE MUSIC LOVER'S GUIDE TO
SERIOUS MUSIC OF THE 20th CENTURY

HOW TO LISTEN TO MODERN MUSIC WITHOUT EARPLUGS

DAVID E. WALDEN

DEAD
COMPOSER

Sound And Vision
Toronto

Contents

* Lucetta lost Chapters 9 *and* 10 and is still looking for them but I couldn't wait.

Foreword

The story goes that the legendary English conductor Sir Thomas Beecham was asked if he had conducted any music by Stockhausen. The reply came, "No, but I once trod in some."

Like all genuinely serious subjects, modern music is ripe for humour. Musicians everywhere have stories to tell about the strange and bizzare things they are asked to do by composers. Nobody is more amusing about music than musicians — witness this book, which incidentally, you should buy, as you are being eyed by a store detective who fully expects you to walk away with it. Why? Anyone interested in modern music arouses suspicions.

A favourite anecdote of mine concerns the trumpeter in the BBC Symphony Orchestra in London, England, who embarking one day upon yet another contemporary work, said in a drawling London dialect "What was this piece called last time we played it?"

In Winnipeg, at an orchestral rehearsal for the first *du Maurier New Music Festival* in 1992, one of the musicians asked "Maestro, do you really like this stuff?" As a matter of fact, I do. I have always been intrigued, challenged, extended, fortified and seduced by the best in modernity.

I belong to that category of musician that does not really care if the audience likes it or not. Of course, if you believe that, you'll believe anything.

But if the truth be told, I have often been amused, annoyed, infuriated, baffled and astonished by many composers and their music.

At *The Winnipeg Symphony Orchestra's du Maurier New Music Festival Canadian Composers Competition* (a title that's eluded many a radio announcer — and from 2000 it will be even longer: *The Winnipeg Symphony Orchestra's Centara Corporation New Music Festival with the major support of Investor's Group, Canadian Composer's Competition*) we made it a house rule that composers were never to be given the microphone in front of the live audience unless they were being interviewed. That way they could be interrupted legitimately. How many of us have been to a new music event and listened to acomposer trudging through a barely abbreviated version of a doctoral thesis (complete with verbose technicalities) that sounds as if the music had been through some kind of committee process before arriving on the platform?

No, that won't do.

There is a very good English word for such an activity. Unfortunately, it is falling out of use because of more picturesque associations — humbuggery. My *Chambers Dictionary* defines 'humbuggery' as "hollowness, pretence." One who so imposes is a humbugger. What a great language we have at our disposal!

David Walden highlights much of the humbuggery of modern music but with a wry humour and a beady eye for the absurdities around which it is all based. For example, look at Chapter 16 and its listener's guide, "From O.K. to Wacky to Way Out."

I was amused to realize that within the last three months I have broken bread or quaffed ale with a composer named in each of these categories. (I suppose that's what they mean by 'eclectic' tastes.)

Yes, Walden, you're absolutely right. It was easier when the Pope said "Listen Michelangelo ... about the ceiling" As a client from both sides of these arts council panels, I can testify to the frustration of both applicant and juror. How does one decide? As Walden so adroitly points out, there is a technique called "Indeterminancy" in music where a portion of the activity is left to chance. Why not try this in the grant process? Well, as a matter of fact ...

On page 50 Walden deals with Satie's *Parade* and its choreography by Massine. Now, as it happens, in 1976, when I was a junior member of the music staff of the then London Festival Ballet (now the English National Ballet), I was deputed to work with Massine himself on a revival of *Parade*. During that season a great many fine scores were up for grabs but as the youngest conductor in the company I got this one. I had visions of asking Massine why typewriters? Why sirens? Why bother? However, when I saw the aged chorerographer I demurred and thought how lucky I would be if I could make it to his grand old age and still make a living from the extravagances of my youth.

I'm still waiting. In the meantime I think we can all gain a great deal from the perspectives of Walden's humour. It's a very clever book. You will unconsciously pick up a good deal of technical jargon, which can help you in your listening endeavours. Like all great humour, there is a good deal of erudition behind the laughter. Furthermore, I challenge you to read between the lines and try to spot the poor lampooned composers that David Walden really loves.

By appreciating the absurd we can hope to understand the phenomenal.

Who knows? By the time you've read this book you might be ready to give new music another try.

After all, it's now the post-modern era ...

Bramwell Tovey
Winnipeg, Canada
April, 1999.

A DEDICATION

This book is entirely dedicated to The Chezlee, Ont., Parsnip and Arts Fest Central Committee and specifically Edna, Laverne, Uneida, Clevinia, Flo, Wilma and Percival (the current members).

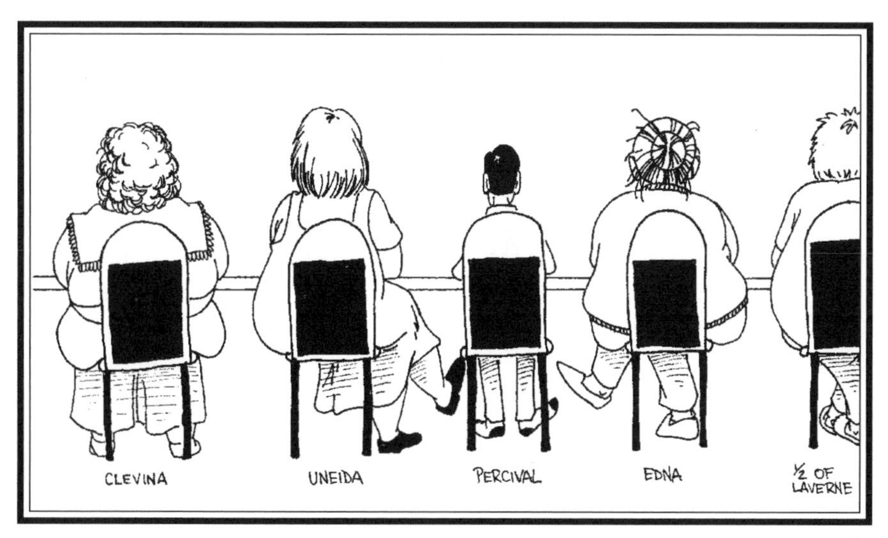

(Flo and Wilma couldn't be fitted in!)

We are blessed in Chezlee, Ont., with their support and encouragement of the performance of musical works by living composers (like myself, the Maestro and Ronnie Fludd, for example).

Asparagus growers, rutabaga distributors, pea-fowl farmers, and emu-burger franchise owners from the environs (to name but a few) eagerly come to the Four Square Gospel Hall on a bimonthly basis, to hear premiéres (and the oh-so-necessary seconderriéres of new works. Their comments and reactions, their items tossed (from cabbages to carnations) are invaluable contributions to the growth of LIVE and MODERN music in the Chezlee, Ont., milieu.

Without the undying support of the Central Committee, none of this would happen and many of us living composers would remain unsung, unheard and unpaid and would be forced financially to seek employment as furrowers, or balers, or stall-muckers, much to our chagrin.

So thanks to the lovely ladies mentioned above (plus Percival) for your contribution to the ongoing development of the pervue of St. Cecilia — namely, MUSIC!

The Author

I NEED NO INTRODUCTION, SHIRLEY*

If there's one thing that riles the Maestro to no end, it is unnecessary and/or redundant repetition. Again, I say, reiteration really upsets him. I have just queried him *vis-à-vis* a paragraph or two of introductory material and he snorted, quite rudely, some unintelligible Teutonic phrase (definitely low Deutsch). This was followed by a yell: "Why the _ _ _ _ don't they just buy your first book — *How to Say Awake During Anybody's Second Movement* — because it's all in there?" With that he promptly stomped off in the direction of the bar-slash-garage and there are such noises emanating from this dual-purpose building as would put the fear of God into any decent man, woman — or sheep, for that matter.

So, unbeknownst to him, I'm going to quickly and quietly slip in the briefest of summaries as to WHO WE ARE just in case you didn't purchase the aforementioned book, so you'll know who we are, where we're coming from, and hopefully where the _ _ _ _ we're going! (at least, as far as this book is concerned).

*This is no typographical error! This is a specific reference to you, Shirley Schuntzz! You may have worked at the Chezlee Cheez Factory for years and you may have pretended to be artistically sophisticated, but the only culture you have is in your yogurt! We have been introduced at least six hundred thousand gazillion times and yet you still wanly ask "Have we ... ah ... met?" Well, we have, Shirley, and I'm sick of it! Get glasses or get lost. You know darn well who I am. And you have no reason to adopt a high and mighty air (unless Limburger qualifies as a cultural status symbol). But enough of that.

PROF. ANTHON E. DARLING B.S.

Me

Professor Anthon E. Darling, B.S., a graduate of B.S.U. in Chezlee, Ont., where I compose, write, instruct, decompose and engage in semi-agricultural activities such as asparagus-stalk shredding and rutabaga rooting, but most of all simply bask in the galactic tutelage of my mentor, namely

Him

Maestro Colli Albani, L.C.B.O., eminent academe and musicological master — a conductor, composer, lecturer and the effervescent container of gallons of knowledge and insight on music and the arts. To boot, he is a bon-vivant who culturally and intellectually towers above the pedestrian milieu of

Chezlee, Ont

the semi-rural community where, in a bucolic setting, the raw delights of nature intermingle with the refined odors of art and music producing a colourful kaleidoscope of cultured and cultural pleasures that stretch from cow patties to *Claire de Lune*. And the specific locum out of which we operate, we nudgingly call

Obscuria

Our modest domain, with its barn-slash-garage, its humble acreage, plopped on the outskirts of town, near Scribbler's Silo, where the Maestro, myself and

Lucetta Teagarden

live. Lucetta is our able-bodied assistant, infrequent pupil, general factotum, constant travelling companion and generally does my typing for me. And I must hasten to say that she does an absolutely stellar job, since some nights, if the Maestro and I have talked into the wee smalls at the Ox & Udder over a flagon or two of Stony Ripple, my notes can tend towards complete indecipherability. How Lucetta makes sense of it all is quite beyond me, so I simply marvel in gratitude.

And so we three live here in rural bliss where creamers and canzonas, combines and concerti, Albinoni and asparagus stalk shredders, fast minuets and fresh manure, St. Cecelia and St. John's Wort enfold our little trio in their arms and provide the perfect setting to pursue the subject of this my second book in the series namely *How to Glisten With Moderate Mucus Without Noseplugs**

*Dear readers, I must hasten to apologize. Lucetta got into the gooseberry wine and, as there is no spell-check on her antique Underwood-Olivetti, the above squiffed title slipped through. Check the title page for the proper name, cause I have to get on with the book ...

AN INTERJECTION: IN MEMORIAMANENSIS

It is with a ton of sincere sorrow that I announce to you all the passing of both Lucy and Maude. Stalwart and brave bovines to the end, they nevertheless succumbed to the mortality that unites us all.

Lucy, alas, one fog-soaked November eve, was mistaken for a crazed copse or fuzzy furze or just an old rock pile by the Maestro himself. He was attempting to aim the dilapidated old Desoto toward the barn-slash-garage that dense dark night after a tense and futile run-through with the Senior Boys Band (average age 83) of the *Polyvetsian Dances*. Their rhythmic thickness and total inability to appreciate the Slavic beat had driven their tireless conductor straight to the Ox & Udder, *aprés*, for a quick nip of Stoney Ripple to numb his offended musical sensibilities. And as he entered Obscuria, between the nog and the fog, he was unable to distinguish the recumbent Lucy from what he thought was a clump of hawthorn bushes. The Maestro never mentions his 'running over' of poor old Lucy although it was with utmost certainty, the single most important cause of his subsequent 'disappearance.' This just-mentioned disappearance I will clear up in a following addendum and put to rest, once and for all, the foul rumours surrounding the incident. But this is a memoriam for two dear friends — creatures of the animal kingdom — and I will not be sidetracked.

Maude, on the other hand, simply and quietly passed on to that great stall in the sky, as she stood in her aged quarters. It was however several days later before we realized that she had gone as her stall was too narrow, and she, alas, too wide. The queer smell that began wafting toward the kitchen door of Obscuria we all at first attributed to Lucetta. That is to say, she was in the midst of pickling her famous rutabaga chips and we thought she got the recipe wrong, (again, I might add). Soon, however, we found Maude's antiquated frame gently falling to dust and gave her a decent bovine burial up under the decrepit Dutch Elm-diseased trunk behind the barn-slash-garage.

Happily, though, our departed beasts have now been replaced by Cliff and Clarice, a lovely old Holstein couple that give us all a great deal of joy and very little milk.

So here's to you, Lucy and Maude. May you be content in your celestial pastures and never suffer from dry teats.

LET ME CLEARLY STATE, RIGHT OFF THE TOP ...

Let me clearly state, right off the top, that I myself am a composer of Modern Music and, as a result, could be accused of having a conflict of interest in writing a book encouraging you, dear reader and lover of our most glorious sound art — namely, music — to listen to Modern Music — namely, MINE!

Well, nothing could be further from the truth. The Maestro — or Colli, as I call him after an evening of one too many Stoney Ripples at the Ox & Udder — has instructed me thoroughly in the discipline of being able to

LIFT YOURSELF ABOVE

the sordid specifics of your own personal miasma and

PRESENT THE LARGER PICTURE

and that's what I will do, dear reader, with complete diffident and indifferent disinterestedness (or else close to it). I'll be probing and prodding with that same fearless searchlight I used in my examination of concert going* so this is

NO SELF-INTERESTED PROMOTION OF MY OWN MUSIC

Second, I hasten to assure you that this in not an

OLD FUDDY-DUDDY DIATRIBE

on "WHY AREN'T THINGS THE WAY THEY USED TO BE? HMMMM???"

No sir! This is

a) a Tribute

b) a Love call

c) a Challenge

d) a Shout from the barn rafters

to

EXPOSE YOURSELF

to Modern Music, that is, and soon you'll be itching to lay down that $6.53 for the best seats in the hall (Four Square) (except for seat 13F 'cause there's a splinter that'll rip more than your Fruits of the Loom) in order to hear the LATEST composition by a LIVING composer, whose ink is barely dry.

I admit, right off the top, that music today is in

A BIT OF A MUDDLE!

There are pieces of music swirling about, that, if they were beef, they would never pass government inspection. They're simply 'off,' or, to put it in other words — Keep your earplugs on!

*entitled: *How to Stay Awake During Anybody's Second Movement***

**Thank you for the letters. Both of them. Except you, Irvin Tornquist. I thought your diatribe was bitter. Typical, but bitter. Tsk, tsk.

HOWEVER,
there are lovely grains of wheat amidst the chaff.

"This is an exciting time," Maestro Colli Albani often reiterates, particularly as the evening wears on. "If your musical tastes stop with Bach or even Brahms and Tchaikovsky, then you simply

HAVEN'T LIVED (MUSICALLY SPEAKING)."

For those of you who read my first tome, I'm sure you remember that pithy epithet given by my distant cousin Millvern Winche at the Chrysler Small Parts Dealers Convention in southwestern Arkansas, when he said:

MUSIC IS A STRANGE BIRD ON A FAR-OFF DISTANT SHORE

Now, this is most assuredly no more true than as a description of Modern Music.

The music of our age has never been as STRANGE

The 'bird of music' has never flown higher or further afield than the music of the age in which we live

And as far as being 'FAR OFF' and 'DISTANT,'

Modern Music, like the human race, has headed to the moon and way beyond.

So let us hoist our petards,
sally forth, take up the torch
and look at, or rather

LISTEN TO

(AND ABOUT)

MODERN MUSIC

AND THE

STATEOFART TODAY

But first, a word

THE MAESTRO'S WHEREABOUTS

I am fully aware that many of you have purchased the present tome you are holding in your hand with the express purpose of finding out something about the music of the 20th century. I hasten to assure you that indeed that is my intention and I shall boldly tackle that very subject forthwith.

However, if you have read my previous opus, you also know that, following the Maestro's stellar — nay, saintly — example, I do not back down from facing hard, cold facts and those unsettling truths that most authors shy away from, through fear, false modesty or guilty consciences.* I will not tolerate that kind of weak-willed shilly-shallying, so I forge ahead where few follow behind.

Let me get to the point:

MAESTRO COLLI ALBANI DID NOT GO TO THE BETTY FORD!

Now, I hope that simple straightforward statement from such a trustworthy source as myself will quell the plethora of queries, albeit mostly local in nature (although a few international eyebrows have been raised in a quizzzical-slash-accusatory manner). So let me put all, near and far, straight *vis à vis* the Maestro's whereabouts.

Due to an infection that set in after the unfortunate butane torch incident behind the barn-slash-garage that occurred whilst writing the ultimate chapter of my last book, the Maestro, for reasons known only to that unparalleled mind (although many feel his Desoto death knell to poor Lucy was a significant factor), nevertheless decided to eschew the modern world of medical science and seek succour from Zephaniah, an enigmatic hag who practices Druidic cures and remedies up north of Stipples Corners in a ramshackle shed at the end of a long-since-cared-for crabapple orchard. Zephaniah's potions are mysteriously, yet powerfully effective for body, mind and spirit and Colli indeed has recovered completely from just about everything that has ever ailed him in his entire life.

Now, as to the various reported sightings of our esteemed magister of the musicological realm from way up the peninsula and as far south as the Motel Dip'n Doze in Brampton, I can only attribute them to the jealous ragings of envious lesser minds wanting, in whatever way they can, to detract

*To whit, the chapter on *Brahms and Gas* in my first book created such a stir within several ecclesiastical presbyteries that only the broad-minded Anglican rector and one old German Lutheran would speak to me for months. All I did was speak the truth about problems we all have (and have heard), but there is a price to pay for honesty and I do miss singing the hymns.

from the Maestro's esteem in cultural affairs, or the madcap hysteria of the masses that see rock stars in shopping malls and the blessed Mother of God in snowflakes in Omeemee.

How shocked was I that even the *Chezlee Sez* — much less some of the scummier yellow journalistic rags such as the *Dornock Knocker* and the *Eugenia Exposé* — actually printed reports of people seeing our unsurpassable professor of St. Cecelia's purview, baying at the moon near the Wiarton hotel or running starkers through post harvest corn fields on the outskirts of Leamington. Needless to say, these reports are highly erroneous or certainly grossly exaggerated. Zephaniah's cures do pack quite a whallop and I know many G.P.s who are jealous of her unequalled record of success, but to stoop so low as to spread false rumours — Really!

The Maestro has returned to perfect health in matters corporeal and that Smithsonian-bound mind is as active as ever and ready to tackle our current topic of Modern Music. I will admit there are a few *tabula rasa*'s (slates wiped clean) during the Zephaniah period that even Colli admits he's fuzzy about and where he picked up those cerise patent-leather stiletto-heeled pumps and that tri-pronged leather and lace thing I will never know. But honestly now, I ask you, does it matter? Really?

What we are about to reap from that matchless mind concerning the topic of *How to Listen to Modern Music Without Earplugs* surely outweighs any accidental peccadillos that may have occurred in the danger-strewn path of seeking health and healing.

What

NO ONE ELSE HAS DARED TO TACKLE

we now pursue.

Read, listen and marvel as that titanic 100-proof Italianate mind peels off the layers of mystery surrounding the onion of 20th-century music to reveal the kernel, the bean, the nut, the pearl in the oyster that has

NEVER BEFORE BEEN REVEALED.

CHAPTER 1:
WHY DO MOST PEOPLE HATE MODERN MUSIC ?!

It's a hardcore fact but it's true that neither the Maestro nor I (altho' Lucetta betimes wears lavender-coloured glasses) are ones to slip and slide away from bold realities.

I think this stems from our involvement with nature in this bucolic milieu in which we live, forcing us to mimic nature's own honesty. If, in the course of a meander through our verdant pasture, one foot, or the other, happens to inadvertently step into a pie of 'bovine's best,' there is no point in trying to deny it later when you're sitting at the Chezlee Cabbage and Cultural Cribbage Night *fête* and it becomes obvious that you didn't get it all off.

So let's be honest!

Without really knowing that much about it, most people

a) IGNORE or

ii) LOATHE AND DETEST

serious music of the 20th century. Although I hasten to congratulate you, dear reader, for taking the big step and making a start by buying my book.

And I must say I have never heard more emotional outbursts than the average person's reaction to a piece of modern music.

I have seen regular church goers nod and slumber in their pews while the most heretical nonsense has been being spewed forth from the pulpit and still drop their sheckles in the collection plate. Yet try, as a living modern music composer (myself, for example) to get one of your latest pieces performed at the Four Square Hall and the subsequent uproar and demands for refunds makes the 100 Years War look like a tea party.

I would like to provide you with a list of comments that I myself have personally heard not only following but during the première performances of pieces of modern music.*

THINGS I'VE HEARD PEOPLE SAY, BOTH DURING AND AFTER A MODERN MUSIC PERFORMANCE:

1) It's just a load of garbage.
ii) ... pile o'crap ... pile o'crap ...
c) Cotton batten wouldn't work, so I used my socks.
4) Why can't composers leave well enough alone! What's good for Mozart's good enough for me.
(V) Why ... Why ...Why do they do it?
(f) It's the musicians I feel sorry for. They're the ones who have to play that junk.
(VII) It all sounded like one massive orchestral gastric attack — and now, as a result, I've got one!
(h) If they think I'm going to pay $7.32 for the best seats in the house, to sit and listen to that ...
(9) I've heard better sounds from the barn!
(X) "I've never believed in a personal devil or the existence of evil until tonight. Satanic forces were unleashed on our eardrums. Years of penance could not atone for what Mr. A._ _ _ _ _ _ _ subjected us to this evening."

(A direct quote from the *Chezlee Sez* about you-know-who's premiere of a work called *Duet for 2 Cream Separators.*)

What I am saying to you, dear reader, is this:

I UNDERSTAND AND ACCEPT YOUR HOSTILITY

But let Colli and I grasp your musical hand, fill in the blanks of your musical mind, take out those plugs from your musical ears and

EXPLAIN
INFORM
BRIDGE THE GAP

*I encourage any underage children at this point to go make themselves some Freshie or purchase a popsicle, as some of the remarks are rude if not incendiary.

BETWEEN

MODERN MUSIC and YOUR'S AND THE GENERAL PUBLIC'S EAR

So that, having EXPOSED YOURSELF and hopefully LISTENED TO IT. You may even begin to LIKE IT.

To share a personal confession with you, I used to absolutely loathe and hate:

1. olives
2. the new minister at the Chezlee United Brethren Episcopal
3. Wagner
4. certain pieces of Bruckner, Albinoni and Haydn
5. Lima beans
6. Elmer Eebles's pit bull terrier and
7. creamed corn from a can.

But, you know, in time, through trial and error, and frequent exposure, I have learned to love all of the above (with the exception of Nos. 3 & 6 and both of them are now dead so who cares?)

Soon, you too, will be saying things like:

"You know, the Brandenbergs are beginning to lose me and *The 9th* I've heard so often, I think tonight, I'll listen to

Lutoslawski's *Silesian Tryptych* or Stockhausen's *Gruppen* or maybe even

Prof. Anthon E. Darling's *Trio for Bass Clarinet, Butter Churn and Autoharp* [Op. 4(b)].

CHAPTER 2:
WHAT IS MODERN ANYWAY?

One late August eve, as the Maestro, Lucetta and I wound our way through old man Brumble's Bough (pronounced — and smells like — bog) returning from a stirring première of a new piece called *Ova-Nova* — an intriguing work by Merzy Fhigmolle, a local turkey farmer/composer — Lucetta, our able-bodied assistant and constant travelling companion, suddenly turned to Colli and me and asked, diffidently:

LUCETTA IN THE MUD HOLE

"What is Modern anyway?" and promptly fell into a stagnant, fetid, thicket-hidden mud hole, as she wasn't looking where she was going. It wasn't until much, much later, in the wee hours of early morning as we sat 'neath the dry, cracked branches of the dead Dutch Elm behind the barn, airing Lucetta's drenched apparel and thus blacking out a considerable amount of moonlight, that the Maestro — musicological wizard of the ivory tower — was able to respond to Lucetta's tossed-off then bogged-down query.

"Modern is as old as the hills, Lucetta," started off the Maestro. and with that she fell into Somnia's arms, wrapped tightly in Cliff's or Clarice's winter blanket.

"Go on!" I urged immediately, as Colli can be a bit sensitive to audience-dozing, and the notes I subsequently scratched down on a whitewashed board of the compost shed form the basis of this chapter.

"Modern is as old as the hills, and I mean that in both senses," Colli, went on, grateful for the Stoney Ripple libation I'd provided.

Firstly: What we call Modern Music is really quite old, starting, as most music historians generally agree, roughly around 1900.

"You mean Modern Music is almost 100 years old?" I gasped, jaw agape as I reached for another Ripple.

"Precisely," Colli said, belched, then continued. "Do the map, Anthon, the map!"

"I've done it already, Colli, in my first book," I daringly responded.

"Then do it again, YOU GREAT THREE-TOED SOUTH AMERICAN SLOTH!!!

People can NEVER have enough of historical maps. They need to know WHERE WE'VE BEEN so's they can know WHERE WE'RE GOING, otherwise we're LOST LOST LOST! (Bang)."

(The capital letters indicate the volume the Maestro attained during this outburst and the 'Bang' reveals the force with which he hit the dead Dutch Elm's trunk, causing all of Lucetta's not-yet-dry apparel to fall in a clump on top of her. Fortunately her slumber was deep and she didn't notice till morning).

Needless to say, I feel compelled to repeat the map from my earlier tome with apologies to those of you who did nail the previous one to the back of your lavatory doors and memorized it thoroughly (particularly during that dreadful intestinal flu outbreak in early March).

Here 'tis, The Map of the HISTORY OF MUSIC:

1725 Rococco 1775

1000	1450	1600	1750		1825	1900
Gregorian	Medieval	Renaissance	Baroque	Classical	Romantic	Modern

As you can clearly see from this map, Modern Music starts circa 1900 and here we are circa 2000. We've been in the period of Modern Music for almost 100 years, and yet we're still grimacing, turning up our noses and shoving down our thumbs about 'this Modern crap' and it's

REALLY QUITE OLD!

I think it's time we got on with it! Don't you?

Amazingly, Lucetta awoke at this point, for, from under the pile of still-bog-soaked garments, a voice was heard:

"If it's been around that long, how come most of us still don't like it? Has this past 100 years simply been the Limberger Cheese period of music, and we should just throw it out, like that blood pudding that went off last October, and start afresh?"

To say that the Maestro 'hit the roof,' in an *al fresco* setting, would be somewhat incredible, but the height achieved by a flock of old crows that had been resting on the upper twigs of the dead Dutch Elm when Colli bellowed should have been recorded in Guinness's. Essentially he said "No!" and "Wait and See!" and then continued, albeit hoarsely:

In the Second Place, the whole question/controversy of "Modern" versus "the way we've always done it" has been going on for centuries.

And here, dear reader, I must doff my hat and salute our illustrious Magister of Music. With his vast grasp of the past, his rapid recall of comprehensive detail and his staccato delivery, he nipped through the centuries, picking out the plums of the NEW versus OLD debates and spread them before us like an abundant harvest cornucopea.

I have now spread for you, what was spread for me in summary:

FIRST F'RINSTANCE
TIME: 1325
NAME OF THE BOOK: *SPECULUM MUSICAE*
AUTHOR: JACOBUS OF LIEGE

Now, what old Jacobus does is talk about the old music of the previous century, calling it rigid and old-fashioned and labels it as

ARS ANTIQUA*

*This is not a footnote, but more of a bellybutton note because it's much higher up on the page and it has to do with PRONUNCIATION. When you say the word 'ARS' you should really make it sound more like 'ARZ.' The Professor *non-pareil* got into a terrible row with the Reverend McDudd of the __________ Church, when, in the middle of a heated debate regarding which tune to use for hymn number 253, Colli muttered something about the ARS ANTIQUA and, due to a certain cybillance produced by righteous indignation, the Reverend misunderstood the Maestro and responded "You call me an old arse and I'll ..." Modesty and a certain concern for the preservation of presbyterian propriety prevents me from continuing with Rev. McDudd's quote. Suffice it to say that you can get yourself into a major pickle if you don't get your ARZ right!

Having tagged the music of the previous generation as the ARS(z) ANTIQUA, Jacobus de Liege went on to say that the music of his time (the Roaring 20s of the 14th century), should by contrast be called ARS* NOVA or ARS* MODERNORUM. (*Same thing as before: Say ARZ or you could get your ARS in trouble.)

"You mean to say there was Modern Music way back then?" I can hear querying down the halls of your mind.

Absolutely! And let me here re-create a paragraph describing the music of this period. I've omitted a lot of the detail (cause it's boring) but just get a whiff of the words used to describe this "Modern" music of 1325:

There was ... SECULARIZATION ... greater REFINEMENT and EXPRESSIVENESS ... a FREE contrapuntal texture ... with SUPPLE rhythms ... and CURVED lines ... MORE THIRDS ... BOLD use of SYNCOPATION ... and UNPARALLELED COMPLEXITY.

Well land o'Goshen, if that doesn't sound like a description of Modern Music, I don't know what does, and this stuff is so old, I'll bet none of youse has ever even heard it once in yer life.

And it happened AGAIN.

SECOND F'RINSTANCE
TIME: 1602
TITLE OF PUBLICATION: *NUOVE MUSICHE*
COMPOSER: GIULIO CACCINI

Giulio published a bunch of songs under the title *Nuove Musiche* (*New Music*) and established one of the most important landmarks in the history of music. Along with the much-more-famous MONTEVERDI and the not-quite-so-famous PERI, old CACCINI gave birth to:

a) the Baroque Period (1600-1750 or 1725)

2) the birth of OPERA
ORATORIO
CANTATA

iii) the concept that "The text, should be the master of the music, not the servant."

Once again, in the history of music, they talked about the old polyphonic style of PALESTRINA that was out-worn and dated, and contrasted it with the new, modern style. Needless to say, there were horrendous fights between the old guard and the *avante* guard and there was even a HEATED CONTROVERSY!

Monteverdi:	**Artusi:**
father of the opera	**old fuddy-duddy theory**
champion of the new	**teacher, champion of the old**

VERSUS

The battle of quills that went on between these two is no less venomous or heated than any reviews of the premières of yours truly's work in the *Chezlee Sez*, written by that viper of the press, the insidious destroyer of the products of the musical mind, Irvin Tornquist — and yes I mention you by name, you miserable sod, because you have singlehandedly destroyed the possibility of a second performance of any of my premières and have through your vile and twisted words made them my derrières as well.

However, not wishing to get off the track, suffice it to say that controversy between the new and the old has existed since time immemorial and there really ain't nothin' much new in the universe.

Just at the point when the Maestro had finished a most dramatic representation of the Monteverdi/Artusi controversy and had poked himself rather badly in the left eye with an electric cow prod, one of the sheep, awakened by the gruff and vicious shrieking of Colli as he lept and yelled from side to side of that anitquitous debate, suddenly bleated ...

Baaaaaaa ... and choked at the end ... *ach*!

"And there's another example! Thanks, Bertha." While this was clearly a reference to Bertha, our prize ewe, I was completely at sea as to where the captain of our musicological ship was sailing.

"What the ...?" I muttered seemingly *sotto voice.*

"Bach, you nimrod! *Bach.*"

"Oh, Bach!" I replied, wincing a bit at his curt and cutting appellation. "But Bach, surely, has nothing to do with Modern Music. Or does it — or rather, does he?"

"Don't call me Shirley," the Maestro fumed and went on, with a certain edge in his voice. "That's exactly my point, you adle-pated unmitigated mental midget!"

At this point, I do have to do some editing of the Maestro's insightful remarks as the pain in his eye from the electric cow prod was increasing, as did his interjected epithets, God bless him. So, once again, for the sake of any Anabaptist readers, I distill the essence:

When we say, "Ahhhh ... Bach ... YES!"

we mean, of course, the great Johann Sebastian Bach (1685-1750), probably the most cranially gifted composer in the entire history of music.

However, let the following facts ricochet through your mental rafters.

1. Bach had 20 kids
2. At least four of them were famous composers:
   a) Wilhelm Friedeman Bach
   b) Carl Phillip Emmanuel Bach
   c) Johann Christian Bach
   d) the other one
3. In their time, when Papa Bach and his boys were all living, it was his sons who were famous, as in "new," "modern," "hip," "with it" composers.
4. Daddy Bach got such descriptions as:
   old Bach
   old fuddy duddy

old-fashioned
old fa_ _!
old organist
old-style composer
old etc.

"So you see," summed the Maestro, "even in Bach's day, the fight between the NEW and the OLD, the MODERN versus the "tried and true," the "what the Hell is going on?" versus the "why can't things just be the way they were?" was going on.

The AMAZING THING is that so-called MODERN MUSIC has been going on for ALMOST ONE HUNDRED YEARS and here I am, humble rural student and practioner of the art of music, having to write a book trying to explain something as old as a century that most people still have difficulty with.

And may I say further, that FEW if ANY have tried to write honestly and forthrightly about MODERN MUSIC with a concern to communicate to the general public and its ear WHAT'S BEEN GOING ON!

I tread where few have dared to tread before. I prod, probe and expose, in order that YOU, DEAR GENTLE READER, may

a) understand what on earth happened almost a hundred years ago
2) understand why most of you reach for earplugs instead of a nice glass of Stoney Ripple Ale to listen to Modern Music
iii) get to the point where you might be able to LISTEN TO MODERN MUSIC WITHOUT EARPLUGS
and
a) listen right thru to the end of it
and
ii) possibly even ENJOY IT!

And that's my task, my *raison d'etre*. So let's to'it.

CHAPTER 3: WHY DO MOST PEOPLE PREFER THE GOOD OLD MUSIC OF THE GOOD OLD (DEAD) COMPOSERS?

Strange as this illustration may seem, it is intrinsically relevant to this current chapter, as you'll soon see.

One sun-strewn evening in late August, that incandescent peeler of the onion skins of knowledge, Colli, explained (with much mirth, I might add) how he was once asked to address the Chezlee, Ont., Bilingual Cross-Stitch and Columbine Club — a delightful gaggle of "fair and forty" damsels who met bimonthly to discuss their slipped-stitch and/or proper fertilizer problems — all *à la française*. The one exception to this distaff exclusivity was Mr. G. D. Phineas, whose French was exquisite and his crochet-work non-pareille, so he was invited as a para-member.

The Maestro had been invited to give a guest lecture on the subject which "les girls" had drawn up, namely:

MUSIQUE MODERNE
MALADE OU MERVEILLEUSE?

which Colli roughly translated (in his own notes) as *Modern Music: Pain in the Arse or Pantheon of Bliss?*

Now, while the bulk of his talk was to have been a discussion pro and con re: modern music, he wanted to start off with a dynamic introduction with his favourite theme, that being "Let's look at the past! Let's look first at where we were, what was going on before Modern Music," and then, he felt strongly, and only then can we understand our present age and its music.

He had searched for a pithy and dynamic phrase with which to commence his lecture, grab their attention and challenge them to "look at the past" before considering the present.

Of the many tongues with which the Maestro was fluent, French was not in the top five and as Chezlee, Ont., was primarily unilingual, his had dropped a bit through lack of usage. (His French, that is).

After an effusive intro by Mme. Jean-aviève Swate (acting President of the C.O.B.C.A.C.C. since 1973 due to the untimely passing of Mme. Loosille Frambwaz from gout-gone-wild), the Maestro strode to the podium, grabbed each side of the make-shift lectern firmly in his stocky agrarian hands and shouted declamatorially:

REGARDE
VOTRE
DERRIÈRE!

Now, the word Colli should have used is HISTOIRE, which is the proper word for "past," as opposed to derrière, which has more the meaning of behind — or, as the ladies misunderstood, their behinds. Had he used *histoire*, perhaps the room would not have cleared quite so quickly (with the exception of M.G.D. Phineas, who remained cowering under his chair and wouldn't come out till well after dark.)

An emergency call from the kindly landlord at the Ox & Udder much later that evening alerted me to Colli's condition due to his chagrin at having cleared the hall so quickly because of his *grande faux-pas*. Thanks to Elmer Eeeble's buckboard, we were able to get him home, and the bulk of this book is based on the notes from the lecture he would have given if they'd stayed after his opening line asking them to look at their behinds.

So, getting back to the point, WHAT IS IT ABOUT MUSIC WRITTEN BEFORE 1900 that causes us to make remarks like the following:

a) Ya know, I really enjoyed that!
ii) His 3rd Movement really moved me!
3. Mozart ... I mean ... honestly now ... I ask you ... isn't he just ... what can you say ... you know what I mean?
d) I would pay double to hear that again!
u) Couldn't you just SEE those French soldiers slugging their way across the Russian steppes? I cried ... I wept ... I ...
6. Bach! It's like listening to a lecture on the binomial theorem. My mind is exhausted. My soul's been probed. My bum is numb but I have been transported.

Well, dear reader, fasten your mental seatbelts and gird up your cranial loins because with the help of the Maestro's notes, I'm going to

SIMPLY and SUCCINCTLY

explain the entire history of Music in Western Civilization from the beginning to circa 1900s so we can in subsequent chapters find out what the _ _ _ _ happened circa 1900 that seems to have blown good music to smithereens and caused the turmoil this present book is dedicated to wiping out. Here goes!

(Before I do, let me just interject a word to those academes and pseudo-intellectual pedants, who are wagging their scholarly appendages and proclaiming such things as "How dare he!?" "What nerve!" and "If he thinks he can simply and succinctly sum up roughly one thousand nine hundred years of music and explain why most people like it, he must be OUT OF HIS MIND."

Well, Colli said it best in the following poem:

If you can't sum it up, you don't know it!
If a child can't understand, you are obtuse!
If your knowledge can't be simple
It's an academic pimple
Squeeze it out!
Clear it off!
It's no use.

— Maestro Colli Albani, L.C.B.O.
(taken from the washroom wall of the Ox & Udder)

FIRST REASON WHY WE GENERALLY PREFER MUSIC PRIOR TO 1900:

1. YOU CAN HUM THE TUNE!

It's true! Oversimplistic, but nevertheless true! And before you scoffers and skeptics go off looking for a blunderbuss to shoot my theory (and head) full of holes, LET ME EXPLAIN.

A. Music started out as a SINGLE LINE MELODY. Like this:

For the first thousand years of the Common Era (1 to 1000), most of the "official" music was called Gregorian Chant, used in the services of the Christian Church.

So you could certainly hum the tune 'cause that's all there was.

B. From 1000 to 1600 (approx.) They started combining MELODIES together. Like this:

This was called POLYPHONY (many sounds) and it was much harder to hum the "tune" on your way home from church, but it sounded lovely.

C. From 1600 to 1900 (very roughly) they started combining a MELODY with HARMONY. (Harmony was three or more notes sounding together. Also called a triad or a chord.) Like this:

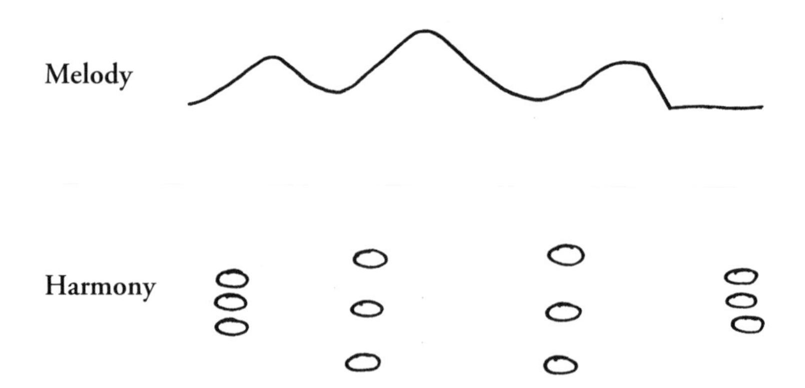

Once again, you could clearly hear the tune and hum it all the way home from church or royal court or even the local pub and, later, public concert halls.

Now it's mostly music from 1600 to 1900 that we lump under the general title

CLASSICAL or SERIOUS music,

(actually 3 1/2 periods: Baroque, Rococo (1/2), Classical, Romantic) and that's mostly what they play on your FM stations or live in your Concert Hall or on C.D.s at your favourite record store.

So, in summary, please remember that with music prior to 1900, somewhere, somehow there's a tune, a MELODY, that, when you're having a shower in the old tin tub in the kitchen with Lucetta pouring buckets of rain water over your head, YOU CAN HUM (and it can be quite pleasant — humming, I mean).

SECOND REASON WHY, GENERALLY, WE PREFER MUSIC PRIOR TO 1900:

2. IT'S RELATIVELY SIMPLE!

(I heard that! I distinctly heard that remark, Irving Tornquist! And it's completely uncalled for and excessively rude, to boot! Just wait and listen and you'll be smirking on your other side!)

The BUILDING BLOCKS OF MUSIC for the first 1600 years were these:

A B C D E F G A (same one repeated higher)

That's it! SEVEN NOTES! Pretty simple, huh?

Now, they did arrange them differently, starting and ending on each of the seven notes. Like this:

A B C D E F G A
B C D E F G A B — These were called MODES
C D E F G A B C — and the music that was written
D E F G A B C D — using them was called MODAL!
E F G A B C D E — i.e. using the SYSTEM of Modality
F G A B C D E F
G A B C D E F G

Then, towards 1600, a couple o' things happened:

First thing: Two modes became really popular:

This one: C D E F G A B C, which they now called the Major Scale, and this one: A B C D E F G A, which they now called the Minor Scale.

Second thing: They discovered five notes in between the seven notes they'd been using. Here:

And, by using these new (black) notes they found 14 different ways of writing the Major Scale and 14 different ways of writing the Minor Scale, which, with the original two, added up to 30 scales (15 Major Scales and 15 Minor Scales). Remember, in actual fact there were only two different scales (Major & Minor), but later on they discovered you could TRAVEL FROM ONE TO ANOTHER. And this was terribly exciting.

Music written using a certain scale was said to be "IN THE KEY OF" that scale eg. Bach's *Sonata in (the key of) G minor* (for harpsichord or flute or old cowbell or whatever he had kicking around). This was called the MAJOR/ MINOR SYSTEM or the SYSTEM OF TONALITY and from 1600 to 1900 (roughly) the music we all know (and love, I dare say) was written using it, and was called TONAL MUSIC.

One more SIMPLE thing: When you listen to music, you usually tap or snap or wiggle or jiggle or nod or MOVE SOMEHOW to THE BEAT!

This is called the RHYTHM of the MUSIC. And for the most part, in music from 1600 to 1900, music was organized in BARS or MEASURES that had either

2 beats: strong weak | strong weak | strong weak
3 beats: strong weak weak | strong weak weak | strong weak weak
or
4 beats: strong weak not so strong weak| strong weak not so strong weak| strong weak not so strong weak

Now, could "time"or rhythm be more SIMPLE than that? (Particularly when you consider that music from India has AS MANY AS 36 beats in a single bar! Think on that as you down a Stoney Ripple or two.)

THIRD REASON WHY IN GENERAL WE PREFER MUSIC PRIOR TO 1900:

3. YOU KINDA KNOW WHAT IT'S ABOUT

Take Art, for example. (No, I don't mean Art Quigmolde, and there are reasons why no self-respecting young woman of Chezlee, Ont., has not taken you up on your nuptial offers but this is not the time or place to deal with that.)

Up until 1900, when people looked at painting or sculpture, they would remark thusly, for example.

a) The Virgin Mary looks right enough but the baby Jesus looks like he's cholic-y!

b) Thank God she's a Queen and has lots of money 'cause she sure ain't a looker!

c) Cows? Is that proper subject material for an artist?

d) Why do they always have to have their clothes off?

e) If that's his idea of Hell, frankly it looks like more fun than the other place.

f) That's a lovely pair of Bougainvilleas she has.

In other words, in painting and sculpture, for about 1900 years, most people in general

KINDA KNEW WHAT THE PICTURE WAS ABOUT!

"So what about Music?" you query. It's roughly the same thing! You have

A. MUSIC based on WORDS. This is sung or vocal music where a certain text is set to music. In most cases the music appropriately "fits" the words — e.g. the music for the *Hallelujah Chorus* for Handel's *Messiah* is kinda Hallelujah Music.

B. Music that Repeats

This is where you have a format or structure like this:

something	something else	something (again)
	or	
A	B	A

There are tons of variations on this principle but essentially when that "something" returns again, you say: "Oh yes! I recognize that!" And you feel kinda good and satisfied and happy to have payed the $5.43 for the tickets.

C. Music based on a PROGRAM

This, as odd as it may seem, is called PROGRAM MUSIC and you can usually tell what it's about from the title, or certainly from the description printed out in the program the usherette gives you on the way to your seat (if she remembers).

If it says: Debussy's *La Mer* (*The Sea*) you can safely assume you'll hear a lot of tossin' and turnin', heavin' and ho-in', ebbin' and flowin' and generally wet music. And, in this case, you sure do.

So IN CONCLUSION combine all three of these reasons:

1. You can hum the tune (sort of)
2. It's relatively simple (kinda)
3. You sorta know what it's about (roughly)

and

THAT'S WHY MOST PEOPLE IN GENERAL, PREFER MUSIC WRITTEN UP TO THE YEAR 1900 (approx.).

Now, we've just gone through an intense section of profound thought, heavy pedagogical thrusts and overviews of two millenia of musical history and I don't know about you, but I'm thirsty! The Maestro has kindly suggested that we head off to the Ox & Udder to down a Stoney Ripple (or 10) and look at the LARGER PICTURE.

"How much bloody larger can you get, Colli?" I demanded of him (somewhat brusquely, I admit).

With that knowing twinkle in his eye, and a rather patronizing lowering of those learned eyelids, he patted me on my somewhat seedy tweed suit jacket shoulder and said,

"We've only just begun."

He paused, then added

"Keep that in mind for a pop-tune lyric. It just might work."

We're off to the Ox & Udder, so there'll be no more writing tonite. Why not head off to your favourite local and — I'm coming! I'm coming! (Impatient *#@!)

CHAPTER 4:
ROMANTICISM BOILS UP AND OVER AND BURNS OUT

Last October, Lucetta was boiling up her Peony Phlox and Passion Fruit marmalade, which always sells well at the Chezlee, Ont., Parsnip and Arts Fest Bake Sale due to its rumoured aphrodisiac properties. But in the midst of her boil, Lucetta suddenly remembered she'd forgotten to give Sue-Louise (our pet sow) her annual bath. Abandoning her batch of marmalade (and her marbles, for that matter) she and Sue-Louise spent the afternoon in the lily pond swamp, frolicking and bathing, and completely oblivious of the turmoil and trauma happening in our kitchen, which I entered only to find a crisp brown/black smudge hardened over the surface of the floor, ceiling and every single kitchen utensil in the room.

Needless to say, her marmalade had BOILED UP AND OVER AND BURNT OUT.

LUCETTA'S BOIL-UP/BURN OUT

As I recalled the incident during recent intercourse with the Professor on the stairs, he said (and I quote): "That's it! That's what happened to ROMANTICISM. Exactly the same thing. It boiled up, boiled over and burned out." Now, the Romantic Period in Music (1825-1900, roughly) was

A LOVELY PERIOD IN MUSIC

All kinds of Romantic "faves" leap to mind and we've all sat there, in the plush velvet seats in the semi darkness, closed our eyes, and been

a) transported to exotic locations
b) had our emotions (and lower) brought to a climax of ecstasy
c) then gently been calmed down to serene tranquillity
d) had the "Divel" scared out of us by spooky music
e) sobbed with joy/sorrow at the heart-tugging strings
f) etc. etc. etc.

But after awhile (I mean this strictly in terms of the period), "Romance" can only go on for so long and you need more than a break and a Craven A.

Now, before we look at Romantic BURNOUT let's consider:

The Three MOST Important SPICY CHEFS of the ROMANTIC SOUP that added that little extra ZEST that led to blowing the lid off the Romantic Movement and causing its BURN OUT.

FIRST OF THE THREE ROMANTIC "SPICE GUYS"

Hector Berlioz (1801-1869), most famous for his *Symphonie Fantastique* and his predilection for BIGNESS in general.

Now, Colli and I identify closely with Berlioz here, as we have always been peculiarly fond of our Lucetta and when it come to BIGNESS, she has the market cornered.

But Berlioz was not only into BIG, he was also into

1. new exotic sounds
2. new combinations and uses of orchestral instruments
3. total rejection of pure or abstract music
4. music MUST represent something beyond mere tones — i.e. PROGRAM MUSIC which, in the case of the *Symphonie Fantastique* was "Scenes from the Dream of an Opium-Drugged Artist!!!"

This is a pretty cool and spicy guy to be cooking up Romantic Music and he certainly broadened the recipe book for Romantic composers to cook from. Why don't you listen to some Berlioz to help you, with the aid of his musical Shoe Horn, slip into the shoe of Modern Music with less pain. Try the *Symphonie Fantastique* on for size. See if you like it.

SECOND OF THE THREE ROMANTIC "SPICE GUYS"

Franz Liszt (1811-1886) — and call him "List," for Pete's sake, otherwise you get into such sizzling sounds you sound like bacon frying on the griddle.

Here was a married priest that women (and some men) grabbed at or swooned over 'cause he moved them so much when he played the piano and yet he was ONE OF THE MOST AMAZING INVENTIVE COMPOSERS OF THE CENTURY! AND A POWERFUL INFLUENCE.

His chromaticism was as free as his morals. His dissonances made him sound "Modern." He's as tough to listen to as 20th-century Music. But he was, without doubt

THE TABASCO SAUCE OF ROMANTICISM.

Why not listen to his *Faust Symphony* or his *Dante Symphony*?

For those of you with sensitive G.I. tracts, take a good aural antacid pre-listening. But once again, it will whet your appetite for the music of the future that was soon to come, but which is pretty old now.

THIRD (AND MOST IMPORTANT) OF THE THREE ROMANTIC "SPICE GUYS"

Now before we get into him (musically speaking, that is) there are a number of riders and provisos and codicils that need to be outlined, signed, sealed and delivered before we can proceed:

1. Most everybody, now and then, feels pretty hotly, one way or the other about him.

2. In his day, he was regarded as a GOD.

3. G.D. Phineas still does regard him as such so I know he's going to be terribly upset by some of the things I'm going to say about him and run off to his aunts and weep all over her antimacassar. But all I can say to him is: Truth must out, so start running!

4. Many regard him as one of the primary causes of the First, if not the First and Second World Wars, although he is generally considered to be the most important composer of his century.

5. Debussy hated him and made fun of him in the middle of his (now considered racist) *Golliwog's Cake Walk*.

6. G. D. Phineas's aunt just called, complaining of a soaked anti-macassar andit's all my fault! See? I told you.

7. Most of his early works were box-office failures, which I guess, is why I have a certain sense of identification with him.

8. He wrote a great deal about music, most of which is now considered, to quote my mother's friend Beryl, "just a bunch o'garbage."

9. In answering the question "DOES IT SEEM LONG?" when listening to one of his works, the answer is an unqualified "YES!"

For those who haven't guessed, his name is

Richard Wagner (1813-1883) and it is pronounced *Vah*-gnurr not *Wag-ner*. He's German! (And Rick-ard, too, not Rich-ard, for the same reason.)

There is so much to be said here that I have had two Bic pens and three H.B. pencils droop over in exhaustion at the mere thought of being used to write out my thoughts on this titan.

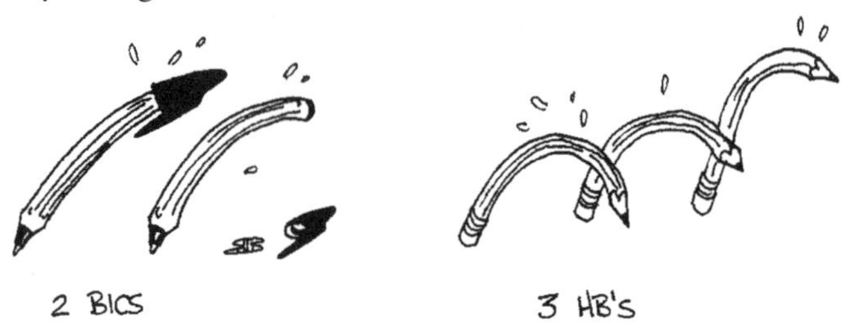

However, in terms of being one of the MAJOR SPERM DONORS to the birth of Modern Music, Wagner is high, if not highest, on the list.

"Why?" you ask? "Why indeed!" I respond.

As I paused to reflect on how best to communicate the answer to that question, Lucetta wandered into the study with that glazed look in her eye that she gets periodically ever since she fell off the roof the other year, and said "I don't know where I am" and meandered out off the porch down to talk to Sheila, her favourite ewe, in the pen.

"That's it!" I cried, with a kind of Archimedes-in-the-bathtub 'Eureka' to it. "That's it!"

I DON'T KNOW WHERE I AM!

"How on earth could 'NOT KNOWING WHERE YOU ARE' be an earth-shatteringly significant contribution to the development of Modern Music?" I hear you querying, dear reader, and good of you to ask.

Remember the GOOD OLD MUSIC OF THE GOOD OLD COMPOSERS long dead?

that was in a certain KEY (like C major)
and it started in C major
and it ended in C major
and you KINDA KNEW WHERE YOU WERE?
Well, Wagner's music can be described as
IN CONTINUOUS FLUX
or CONSTANTLY MODULATING
or TONALLY UNSTABLE
or AMORPHOUS AND CONFUSING

or SATURATED WITH DISSONANT CHROMATICISM.

Or, in other words,

YOU HAVEN'T THE VAGUEST IDEA IN H _ _ _ WHERE YOU ARE!

Oh sure, you're swept up, nay engulfed, in a sea of overwhelming, unending passion that churns your emotions from crests to depths, wallowing in the intensity of feelings. Sure! But Where are you? In C major or F# minor or Saturn or Uranus?

WHO KNOWS?

Listen to the Prelude to Wagner's opera *Tristan and Isolde* (or *und*, if you're German). Go on! Do it now!

Whenever I listen to it, I'm reminded of old Josiah, the Chezlee, Ont., and environs vagrant. He's not slept in the same place twice for 60 years.

"Where do you live, Josiah?" he's been asked hundreds of times by everyone from governmental officials attempting to label, code, tax and expel him, to those with genuine Christian concern for his welfare. The answer is always the same. "Around," replies Josiah with a kind of knowing, patient grin that seems to imply he's better off than the rest of us.

The Prelude to *Tristan and Isolde* is EXACTLY LIKE JOSIAH'S LIFE.

The Prelude goes AROUND!

It starts off as if it's going somewhere, then

It goes around everywhere, then

It ends as if it's going somewhere else!

YOU DON'T KNOW WHERE YOU ARE!

And this was revolutionary! Because, of course the question is "If we don't know where we are ...

WHERE DO WE GO FROM HERE???"

After Wagner, what next???

The Maestro has just suggested "A stiff Stoney Ripple" and I couldn't agree more, 'cause it's been a rough row to hoe, as it were.

Just as, near the beginning of the century when Beethoven wrote his last symphony, the mighty *Ninth*, and every decent, self-respecting composer put his or her (Clara Schumann among others) quill-pen down and said, "Well, that's it! What could possibly be next?" — so, at the end of the 19th century when Wagner FINALLY stopped writing *Der Ring das Nibelungen* (a four-evenings-worth opera — talk about Titanic!) and quietly passed on (altho' there was great hullabaloo and a funeral service on a par with a Queen's (or King's, as the case may be), composers gathered amongst themselves, saying:

"Where do we go from here?"

or "How can we be new or original after that?"

or "He's wenched it dry!"

or "I couldn't possibly think of what to compose now, so I think I'll open a pizza parlour."

But not all composers felt like this, and it's these brave adventurous souls we're going to look at in the next chapter.

It's true! It's not a typo! I don't mean MONSTER! BEETHOVEN WAS A "MODERN" COMPOSER!

Before you say or do anything else, such as

a) say Tsk, Tsk or Pshaw!
b) slam the book shut and go for cappucchino
c) write letters of protest to my publisher
d) speak ill of me at intermission

GO DIRECTLY AND LISTEN TO THE *GROSSE FUGE Op. 131* — the last (alas unfinished) string quartet that Beethoven wrote, in 1826 just before his death in 1826.

GO ON! I'M NOT WRITING ANOTHER WORD UNTIL YOU'VE LISTENED TO IT!

Now, do you see, or rather HEAR, what I mean? It was almost 100 years later before the world again heard sounds like that! I know some of you smarty pants are going to say that the old geezer was deaf as a post at this point and obviously couldn't hear what he was writing!

"Balderdash!"

Colli just read that last line over my shoulder and shouted the above so loudly that Lucetta has fallen into the washtub, where she was laundering antimacassars, and Bythynia, our domesticated sow, just did her business all over the old pantyhose rug that my Aunt Mabel twisted for us last Christmas. But his point is well taken!

Beethoven knew exactly what he was doing! Like the great titan he was, transitional genius, conquering the Classical and rampaging the world into the Romantic, in his last breath he looks into the distant future of the Modern era and gives us a hint, a breath, a touch of THAT WHICH IS TO COME.

Colli has always worshipped Beethoven (and, frankly, just between us, has fancied himself to be a kind of 20th-century version of him. His somewhat slovenly personal habits are an exact replica of his Teutonic model, and though he hasn't written *a Ninth Symphony* yet (as a matter of fact he's only 1/4 of the way through his *First*), he does admittedly look messy.

Also, he does treat me like the son he never had, just like Beethoven treated his nephew Karl, whom Beethoven drove to rescue in the pouring rain and got a cold and died, although in our case it's been me that's picked up the Maestro (more than once, I might add) in the ditch just past the Ox & Udder when Stoney Ripples have blurred his vision and judgement as to exactly where the *#%! road was. What was I saying? Oh, yes:

I'm sure that, having listened to the *Grosse Fuge*, you will, with me,

1. Marvel at Beethoven's progressiveness.
2. Not get quite so snotty about this "modern crap" and say things like "I much prefer Beethoven to Bartok!"
3. Have an open mind (or ears) to listen to more Modern Music and not be so bloody antiquated in your musical outlook.
4. Never again say "All good music died in 1750 with Bach," like the organist at St. Wilma and St. Wodger's Anglican (High) Church, whose musical palette of organ music is as limited as his fashion sense! Imagine! Tweeds on Trinity Sunday! Really!

CHAPTER 5:
TWO ODDBALLS AND ONE (UNKNOWN) INSURANCE CEO

For those of you familiar with Chezlee, Ont., and its environs, you know that from the BAY, the water flows into the SOUND and then into the SYDENBURGH RIVER and then into three tributaries. And they are:

1. the continuing Sydenburgh River, which calmly and straight-as-an-arrow ponders on down the township.
2. the Pottlewattlemot tributary, which twists and turns through Stoney Ripple Township looking for somewhere to flow and finally ends up in McClutcheon's Slough and Bog.
3. the Walmers Falls tributary, which starts rushing headlong to Walmers Falls itself, crashes down hundreds of feet in a churning foamy torrent and heads off at a right angle due north up the peninsula towards the Point!

Amazingly, dear reader, this river resembles exactly what was happening to music around 1900.

First, a map of the Sydenburgh:

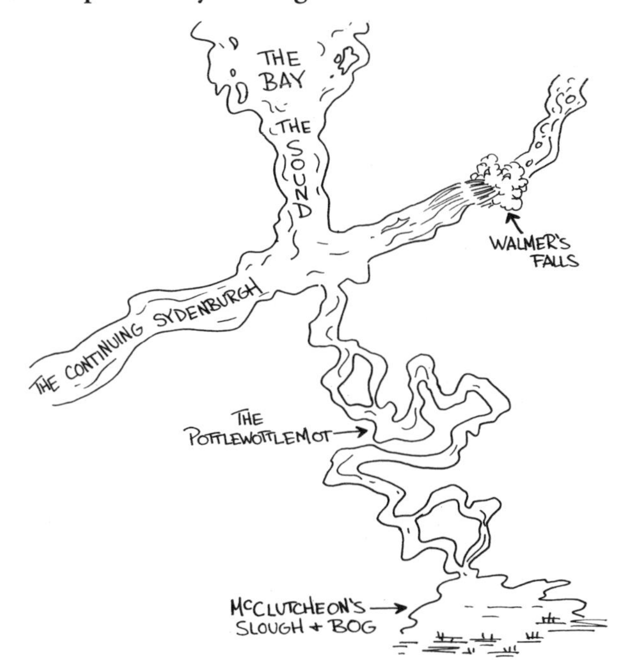

Now, let us look at the BIG RIVER OF MUSIC

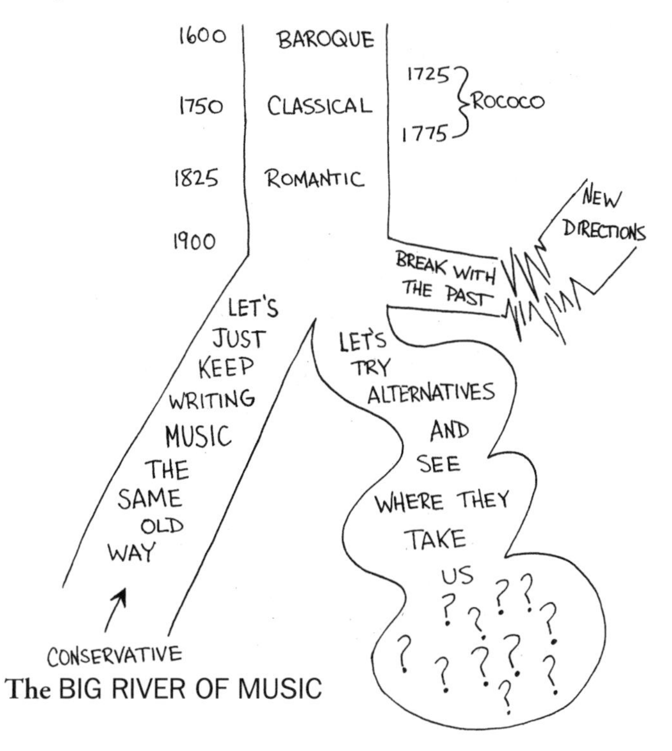

The BIG RIVER OF MUSIC

In this chapter, we will take a glimpse at three composers (two oddballs and one unknown insurance CEO) who represent the second tributary, or those who were SEEKING ALTERNATIVES TO THE WAY MUSIC HAD BEEN FOR 300 YEARS.

FIRST ODDBALL

Alexander Scriabin (1872-1915). How much I identify with this unfortunate Russian who was looking for alternative ways to express his inner musical longings, for he was HISSED, dear reader. He was HISSED!

How familiar that sound is to my own unfortunately sensitive ears. Sixty-three percent of my own premieres at the Four Square Gospel Hall have been similarly showered with serpentine sibilants. So I know how it feels, Alexander, I know how it feels.

In the realm of Modern Music, Scriabin is like an usherette showing us our seats in the concert that is about to begin. He didn't create a new system *per se*, but he tore the old one to such shreds that it's almost unrecognizable (hence the hissing).

As he became more and more chromatic and dissonant, he also became heavily involved in theosophy, occultism and various Eastern philosophies. He also began to drink a few too many wee drops of "Absinthe," which, as I know from personal experience can really fry your brains out. He said his music aimed to produce "A GLIMPSE OF HIGHER SPIRITUAL PLANES" and also "I FOUND LIGHT IN MUSIC, FOUND THIS RAPTURE, THIS SOARING FLIGHT, THIS SUFFOCATION FROM JOY."

Well, dear reader, if those comments aren't the result of a little too much of something-or-other, I'm a monkey's uncle. And yet, regardless of the source of his inspiration he wrote some amazing music. His *Poem of Ecstacy* and his Prometheus the *Poem of Fire* are outstanding examples of an alternative-seeker.

Admittedly, he went a bit odd towards the end and gathered a group of disciples around him back in Russia and dreamed of writing a huge symphony that all the peoples of earth would unite together for in one helluva big party. Two thousand white-robed performers would combine the arts of poetry, acting, dancing, colour, perfume and music and the resultant performance of this colossal work would "MARK THE END OF THIS STAGE OF HUMAN CONSCIOUSNESS."

Scriabin never got around to writing this GIGANTIC MULTI-MEDIA HAPPENING, as he lost his own human consciousness due to blood poisoning from an abscess on his lip. (Reminds one of Jean Baptiste Lully, who got gangarine from stomping his conductor's staff on his big toe and subsequently died. Music's a dangerous business!)

But the music Scriabin did write inspired such comments as:

1. "destined in the future to occupy a niche of their own"

or 2. "the chief advance in musical consciousness since Beethoven"

or 3. "the veritable wind of the cosmos itself**

or 4. "too erotic for my taste" (another eminent composer)

Now, if 1 to 3 haven't whetted your appetite, surely 4 will drive you to your nearest CD store and pick up some Scriabin and a package of Craven A.

SECOND ODDBALL

Erik Satie (1865-1925) I think the reason I have selected Satie as the other oddball to be looked at is that I have such a great sense of identification with him, as will be obvious from the following quotes about him from his peers and colleagues (the capitals are mine to indicate my personal identification with him):

Igor Stravinsky said :

"He was certainly the ODDEST PERSON I have ever known, but the most RARE and consistently WITTY, too."

although Stravinsky also said:

"Who can stand that much REGULARITY?" referring to Satie's steady, plodding, persistent, simple rhythms.

Jean Cocteau said:

"Satie teaches SIMPLICITY ... enough of clouds, waves, aquariums, waterspirits and nocturnal scents; what we need is a MUSIC OF THE EARTH."

Cocteau also said:

"Satie leaves a clear road open upon which everyone is FREE to leave his own imprint ... the Music Hall, the circus, American Negro bands ... all this is as FERTILIZING to an artist as life itself."

Now, if we collect all the words said about Satie and string them together in a line:

ODDEST PERSON, RARE, WITTY, REGULARITY, SIMPLICITY, OF THE EARTH, FREE and FERTILIZING,

you get a list that could not better describe both the music and the life of both the Maestro and myself, as many of these adjectives have been oft used to describe us.

Satie was anti just about everything in music from 1600 to 1900 and while some considered his music the "naive musings of an eccentric dilletante" (words often used to describe my own attempts), many do not and regard

(**I suffered from that the other night and Lucetta and the Maestro asked me to leave for a while so I know what they're talking about!)

him instead as at least influential if not downright innovative.

My overwhelming need for succinctness and organization forces me at this point to share a LIST of salient and shaking facts about Satie that will undoubtedly raise him several notches in the oddball category and send you out to listen to something other than his too-well-known *Gymnopedies* (a title for which there is no translation, so never mind).

1. Here are the names of some of his compositions.
   Three Pieces in the Shape of a Pear
   Dried Embryos

2. In 1917, he wrote *Parade*, with sets by PICASSO, choreography by MASSINI and scenario by COCTEAU. Among the instruments used are:

   a Lottery Wheel
   a Pistol
   a Typewriter
   2 Sirens
   a "Bouteillophone"
   and *Flaques Sonores* (sonorous puddles)

   Furthermore, one of Picasso's costumes was 10 feet tall. The music has been described as

   SIMPLE, HUMOROUS, OUTLANDISH & SHOCKING

3. When he died there were ONE DOZEN CORDUROY SUITS (identical) hanging in his closet, all un-worn! Now what does THAT tell you???

4. He invented "*musique d'ameublement*," or furniture music. This was music he wrote to be played during the intermissions or *entre'acts* of a play. Five players were spread about the hall and the audience was specifically instructed in the program to:

   a) attach no importance to the music
   b) behave as if it didn't exist
   c) keep talking, laughing, drinking, whatever and don't applaud when it's over.

   Unfortunately his experiment failed because the audience listened. But the next time you're in a dentist's office, department store, or elevator of a higher-class condominium, remember that the bland MUZAK that is being shoved down your earhole involuntarily was first called furniture music and was invented by Erik Satie almost 100 years ago.

5. In a ballet called *Relache*, Satie, with the Dadaist artist PICABIA, made a film shown during intermission in which:

   a) Picabia and Satie fire a cannon off the roof of the Louvre and

b) a hearse is drawn by a camel around a five-foot miniature of the Eiffel Tower.

6. Satie had six disciples called *Les Six* and if you can name all six, as well as all seven dwarfs, and send me a self-addressed stamped envelope, I will send you one of Lucetta's pressed pansies. (Hint: you'll find them listed somewhere else in this book and to start you off, my fave is Poulenc. So there's one step on a route to a pressed pansy for you.)

I end the discussion of ODDBALL NUMBER TWO (a.k.a. Erik Satie) with a not-comprehensive list of things Satie used to write above (and below) (and between) his scores. Needless to say, he's poking fun at some of his forebears in music who would litter their scores with words of guidance. Here's the list:

Assez lent, si vous le voulex bien	Fairly slow, if you don't mind
Comme bête	Like a beast
Corpulentus	Corpulent
Dans le gosier	Down in the throat
Dans la tête	In the head
Du bout de la pensée	With the tip of your thought
Du coin de la main	With the corner of the hand
En blanc et immobile	In white and motionless
Grattez	Scratch
Ignorer sa propre prèsence	To ignore your own presence
Munissez-vous de clairvoyance	Arm yourself with clairvoyance
Ne parlez pas	Don't talk
Ne pas se tourmenter	Don't torment yourself
Ne pas trop manger	Don't eat too much
Ouvrez la tête	Open your head
San s'irriter	Without getting irritated
Sec comme un coucou	Dry as a cockoo
Si vous m'en croyez	If you believe me
Très 'neuf heures du matin'	Very 'nine o'clock in the morning'
Très perdu	Very lost
Un peu cuit	A little cooked
Vèritable Prèludes Flasques pour un chien	Genuine Flabby Preludes for a dog

Now admittedly, these are paper jokes and bear no relation whatever to the music itself, but hopefully it will aroint you to listen to a soupçon of Satie and hopefully, a chuckle or two.

3. AND ONE (UNKNOWN) INSURANCE CEO

Charles Ives (1874-1954) was fired as the chapel organist at Yale because of the "weirdness" of his arrangements and so as a postlude on his last Sunday he played *Praise God from Whom All Blessing Flow* with his fists and then became an insurance agent. He said:

"Assuming a man lives by himself and with no dependants, he might write music that no-one would play prettily, listen to or buy. But — but if he has a nice wife and some nice children, how can he let the children starve on his dissonance? So he has to weaken (and if he is a man, he SHOULD weaken for his children) but his music more than weakens — it goes "ta-ta" for money! Bad for him, bad for music!"

Well, good for Ives, cause he had a nice wife and nice kids so he went to work for an insurance company and by 42 he was the head of the largest insurance company in the U.S.of A. And at night, on weekends, and on vacation he wrote some of the most amazing music, writing down the sounds he heard in his head.

But that's the problem. That's the only place they were heard! And when he started to try to get his works published and/or performed, he got replies like the following:

i) "absolutely too difficult."

ii) "Perhaps, Charles, you should take some lessons in the basic rudiments of music theory and learn how to write properly."

iii) "You're nuts, Ives! Totally crackers."

Dear reader, how often have I myself heard these very words ringing in my ears after a personal première or seen them jaggedly gazing at me on a refusal letter from a Toronto publishing company (un-named, you'll note) when I've mailed down a new manuscript, hoping against hope that they will look favourably upon my musical efforts. But alas ...

I feel such a strong sense of identification with Ives also because after REBUFFS and REFUSALS he retired to his BARN in Connecticut and went on writing the music he heard and wanted to write.

Friends (and I have them too, although shall not mention them by name although you know damn well who you are!) would try to persuade Ives to write stuff that was more "popular" — that people would "like" — "nice" music, etc. etc. etc. To which Ives would wearily respond:

"I CAN'T DO IT — I HEAR SOMETHING ELSE."

Oh dear reader, the responsive chord that phrase resonates in my total being is astounding. I too have been hearing SOMETHING ELSE for years and, in actual fact, have been told I'm from SOMEWHERE ELSE for years as well, but I struggle on.

Ives didn't. He pooped out at 44 (in 1918) and hardly wrote again.

He STOPPED in 1918!

Yet years later, when they started rummaging through his barn, they discovered music that was WAY AHEAD OF ITS TIME and who knew? Who knew? Nobody.

In 1939, at age 65, Ives's piano sonata the *Concord Sonata* was performed and hailed as "The greatest music composed by an American." In 1947, at age 73, his *Third Symphony* won a Pulitzer Prize. Now, he was world famous!

In 1951, at age 77, his *Second Symphony* was performed by the New York Philharmonic. Ives just listened to it on the radio because he was old and, probably quite justifiably, cheesed off, thinking to himself:

"Where the hell were ya when I was young and could have drunk all that champagne before I got reflux-esophogitrus and irritable bowel syndrome? It's just too late! Too late!"

Now, I would discuss his music in details that would blow your mind, however this is not the purpose of this present tone. I would mention a ton of pieces like *Three Places in New England* (1903-1911), or *Three Outdoor Scenes* (1898-1911) or *114 Songs* (1884-1921), but time and space do not permit.

Let me simply end by quoting another American composer, Aaron Copland, who said: He lacked neither the talent, nor the ability, nor the *mètier*, nor the integrity of the true artist but what he most SHAMEFULLY and TRAGICALLY lacked WAS AN AUDIENCE!

If you are not immediately running out to your local discount store to pick up an Ives then shame on you. Put this book down this minute. What are my inane prattlings in comparison with the rich aural treasures that await you?

And here's a little bon-bon to further whet your sound appetite. Ives loved hymns and suddenly in the midst of crashing, clashing dissonance and some of the most radical juxtaposition of different musical ideas, you'll suddenly hear the tubas and trombones blasting out *Are You Washed in the Blood of the Lamb?*

Why, I myself, have laughed, audibly, in the middle of a movement of Ives and when chastised (brutally, I might add — and I didn't expect that of you, P.F. Flamonge) I simply replied:

"What the hell do you think Ives meant us to do? For God's sake loosen your girdle, Flamonge!"*

*Thankfully, this time I wasn't kicked out of the Four Square Gospel Hall and so was able to enjoy many more fascinating movements, although I did downgrade the dynamic level of my chuckled responses to somewhere between *mf* and *mp*.

CHAPTER 6:
THE MOTHER OF MODERN MUSIC (WITH A HITHERTO UNREVEALED, EXPLOSIVE AND SHOCKING REVELATION)

The original title of this chapter was simply THE MOTHER OF MODERN MUSIC and I had pinned it up on Clarice's stall wall as I was removing an annoying thistle from her left shank when the Maestro put his firm agriculturally weathered hand on my hunched shoulder, looked furtively left and right, then scanned the ever-empty barn-slash-garage and muttered *sotto voice* (rare for him, *fortissimo* being his more favoured dynamic level):

"There are tales to be told! Hitherto unrevealed!"

At that point, the offending thistle popped loose, hitting the Maestro square in the middle of his forehead, and the stream of verbiage that flowed from that otherwise objective and academic orifice simply cannot be written down. Suffice it to say it was at the *ffff* dynamic level and involved a plethora of comments I could only conclude were directed towards me, as, apart from Clarice, I was the only one present. It was not until much later that night as we sat under the horse chestnut tree making dried corn husk St. Bridget's crosses that he continued.

And it is with trembling hand that I take up the pen to recount what the Maestro revealed that night, as there are forces, still present in today's world, that could —

— I'm sorry. The Maestro has suggested that I deal with the main purpose of this chapter first, to keep building on the body of knowledge we have been accumulating and add, as an appendix or coda, the shocking EXPOSÉ NEVER BEFORE REVEALED!!! I obey. So let's look at this mother of a composer:

Claude Achilles Debussy (1862-1918)

If Wagner was the major SPERM DONOR of MODERN MUSIC, Debussy (as much as he hated his German counterpart) was the EGG and the WOMB that nurtured the EMBRYO OF MODERN MUSIC and gave it birth, although many of the LABOUR PAINS seem to be endured POSTPARTUM by those listening to this "child of music" they created. But enough of pediatric paraphrase.

Stated simply:

MUSIC 1600 TO 1900 had RULES!
DEBUSSY BROKE THE RULES!

The following anecdote shows clearly the young bugger's rebellious tendencies:

As you may know, there's a chord called a Dominant Seventh Chord and all the rules (1600-1900) said that it absolutely MUST move (or "resolve") — and in a very particular way — to a Tonic Chord, which is nice and restful. That movement or resolution is called a Cadence, and that's the way they liked it. In fact, they liked it so much they called it a Perfect Cadence (also known as V-I, but who's counting?)

Anyway, so there's little Claude Achilles (Debussy, that is) studying at the Conservatory of Paris (called the *Conservatoire de Paris* 'cause it was French), upstairs in one of the practice studios happily (and rebelliously) plunking out a bunch of Dominant Seventh Chords one after another in succession and not following the rule that the Dominant Seventh Chord MUST MOVE TO THE TONIC and it must move there in a certain way, no if's, ands or buts! SHOCKING, ISN'T IT?

The Prinicpal of the Conservatoire happened to be passing by, heard what was happening and flung open the door, demanding angrily:

"D'accord quels règles tu joue au piano? Hmmm?"

(He was French, remember? But here's the translation:

"According to what rules are you playing the piano? Hmmm?" (That last part's the same in both languages.)

And do you know what the saucy little kid replied?

"Le plaisir de mes oreilles!" or "The pleasure of my ears!"

In other words, he was saying: "I like the sound of them, one after another, like that! It's neat!" or "The rules be damned. It sounds nice." (And it does, too. If you're near a piano go try out a bunch of them.) Well, there's a feisty lad fer you, eh?

Little Claude Achilles went on and, as he grew up, he continued to explore with FREEDOM all sorts of possibilities and, after him, MUSIC COULD NO LONGER BE THE SAME. He wrote:

"I love music passionately, and because I love it I try to free it from barren traditions that stifle it. It is a free art — gushing forth — an open-air art, an art as boundless as the elements, the wind, the sky, the sea. It must never be shut in and become an academic art."

Early on, Debussy did get some bad reviews. For example: "At present M. Debussy seems to be afflicted with a desire to write music that is

1. BIZARRE
2. INCOMPREHENSIBLE
3. and IMPOSSIBLE TO EXECUTE"

(Descriptions I've often heard about my own music.) However, in this case the comments were made by stuffy old professors at the *Conservatoire* and soon Paris and France and the world loved Debussy's stuff (as did Gabrielle, Rosalie and Emma, who also loved him, and while they did so subsequently, there was some overlapping!).

Now, I'm not going to say any more about the details of his musical innovations, partly because it would get too technical and also because his music gets on concert programs and radio broadcasts and does not create quite the stir as those composers to whom he gave birth — musically speaking, that is.

Let me simply add two words:

First word: In his series of *Preludes* for the piano, he writes the title of each prelude AT THE BOTTOM, AT THE END, AFTER THE PIECE IS OVER!

How lenient of Debussy, eh? He's saying:

"You listen to it! You think about what this piece is about and what you think it should be called! Now that it's over, here's what I called it. How does that compare? Is that what you thought it should be called? If you had a different title in mind, that's perfectly all right. Everybody's entitled to their own opinion, eh?"

You see, Debussy invented THE MULTIPLE-CHOICE QUESTION as well, as a sort of sideline, but equally "modern" in flavour.

Second word: Maurice Ravel (1875-1937) was 13 years younger, but lived longer (although he went a bit cuckoo at the end, constantly hearing a high, high B*b* on a piccolo in his head). Perhaps it was because of his obsession with clocks (he had a ton of them) and always somewhere in his music you can hear something ticking, or clicking, or bonging. While less radical than Debussy, and a bit more intellectual, his stuff is still "out there" and deserves to be listened to. Go on! Now!

"Now's the time, Anthon."

The Maestro has gently nudged me, urging me to procrastinate no further and "tell the tale that has not been told." To carry out this risky business, I have, with Colli's permission, decided to tell his story, IN THE FIRST PERSON, as he told it to me that night under the horse chestnut tree. Trembling, I commence (but remember, it's the Maestro talking):

"It all started back when I was a teenager. Harold was the bogeyman of Chezlee, Ont. He only came out of the house on Sunday evenings after dark to walk across the railroad bridge to the smoke shop to buy tobacco and rolling paper. We'd hide in a lane across the street and watch Harold and Ted the tobacconist talk for half-an-hour or so, and then follow at a distance, behind bushes or barns, as Harold shuffled back to his house, never to appear till the next Sunday evening. The house where he lived with his aged ma was on a secluded little half-street where my great Aunt Ida also lived and she was friends with Harold's mother.

One day my mother sat me down when I returned from my piano lesson and said that Great Aunt Ida had a favour to ask of me. Thinking that it was a lawn to be mowed or a pickle preserve jar, encrusted with age, that needed opening, I said "Sure! I'll do it!"

But it wasn't that. Mother said Great Aunt Ida had been talking to Harold's ma and Harold wanted to meet me, give me some music and hear me play the piano.

"Harold?! The bogeyman?!" I shouted.

"Colli! None of that!" my mother said. "Harold used to be a concert pianist before the war. He's a very intelligent and gifted man."

"So why does he slobber and dribble when he speaks and only comes out on Sunday nights and looks like he's crazy or something?"

"The war, Colli, the war," replied Mother with that knowing, adult look that said "this is all the information you're going to get at the present moment, it's all you need, and really you're old enough to read between the lines and understand the full implications of what I've said."

Eventually persuaded that it was no less than my Christian duty, I agreed to go. For the first few visits I was terrified out of my adolescent wits, but they became not unpleasant sessions. Initially it was difficult to understand him (because of what "The War" had done to his speech patterns) but through time I became accustomed to him and learned a great deal from him and got a pile of wonderful piano music for free. I would play the latest Bach I was working on, or a Beethoven sonata or a Chopin nocturne, and we would discuss the piece, the composer, the music and have what was increasingly becoming a very enjoyable time.

Enjoyable, that is, until the Debussy incident. My wonderful piano teacher, Miss Crawford, had decided it was time to move on from the Baroque, Classical and Romantic repertoire I had been concentrating on and "look at the Moderns," and as Debussy and Bartok were two of her favourites, we started with them.

Miss Crawford gave me Debussy's *Golliwogs Cake Walk*, explaining that a Golliwog was a little black stuffed doll and even in those times was a little politically incorrect, but I loved the piece and attacked it ferociously. I got it up the fastest of any piece I'd ever learned since trying my Grade VIII piano exam and played it every chance I could get.

Needless to say, it was with great excitement and tremendous pride that I went one Thursday evening to see Harold to play for him — my first Debussy! We hadn't discussed music beyond Brahms so I eagerly anticipated the arduous but, I was sure, dynamic dialogue to come. The events that followed etched themselves on my teenage mind with the deep imprint of a sculptor's chisel that time can never erase.

I played 31/2 bars of Debussy's *Golliwogs Cake Walk* and Harold flew into an uncontrollable rage. He tore my fingers from the keyboard and somewhere in the barely intelligible torrent that flowed from his slobbering lips, I heard the words "No" and "You mustn't ever" and "Don't you know?" He was tearing around the room now, wildly leafing through stacks of music, papers and books, yelling loudly and totally incoherently.

Fear held me immobile as I watched this scene short chronologically but a lifetime emotionally. Finally he found what he was looking for and thrust a small pamphlet into my shaking hands and hollered something that must have been "Read this!" although by now rage had reddened him and his mother had come in because of the shouting. He was crying and his mother told me I had to go as Harold would have to be quiet and calm down. I quickly fled into the evening darkness, ran home in a flurry of fear and never returned to play for Harold again.

That night, in my room, under the sheets with the aid of flashlight, I tentatively opened the little 3x5, 15-page pamphlet with heart-pounding curiosity. It was published by Boswell Publishing Company in 1925 in London and was a well-printed, orderly pamphlet that in no way smacked of yellow journalism.

Page after page, it steadily condemned both Debussy the man and his music. The details of this dual condemnation were sparse but definitely weighted on the side of Debussy the man. Words like sacrilege, profane, abomination, immoral and blasphemous were bandied about continually. The critique of his music was not so much because of his breaking the rules and traditions of the past, but of the evil soul of this man that was expressed in his music. By the time I had finished reading the pamphlet I was shaking with shock and yet piqued with mounting curiosity.

What did he do? I wanted to know details. Was it drugs? Was it some bizarre sexual perversion? What on earth was it, that made this author refer to "that which is well known but of which we cannot speak as it is too vile to" etc. etc.? All my questions remained unanswered and I couldn't go back to Harold's and ask him. He had gotten so appoplectically upset with 31/2 bars of *Golliwogs*, God knows what would have happened if I'd asked him what was the matter with Debussy.

So, I took recourse to the only path available to me and I started that very night. I crept quietly down the stairs, put the practice-pedal down on the piano, making the sounds very soft, and began to play Debussy. I played every piece I could get my hands on. I did it at night or when Ma and Dad were out, as I couldn't help feeling there was something quite wicked about what I was doing although I never knew what — not then, at least.

Even Miss Crawford was unable to unlock the mystery. A very open and contemporary woman she was, for a Chezlee, Ont., spinster piano teacher, and my tale of Harold and Debussy did not deter her from continuing to teach me his works. And I could never shake a slightly naughty feeling when, at my lesson, we worked on a Debussy or the distinct feeling of sheer, exciting evil when I practised the *Preludes* or *La Fille aux Cheveux du Lin* while the parents were at church on Sunday evening.

But I was also troubled with questions. Why was I so fascinated with this composer and his music? Did I too have some perverse character flaw that drew me to him? Was I too Satanically possessed, as the pamphlet had implied, and that's why I was so intrigued? What was it about me (and Debussy) that was so horribly wrong? And, in the meantime, my knowledge and appreciation of his music grew in leaps and bounds, but nowhere in any book could I find any hint of reference to what the pamphlet had stated was virtually universal knowledge a mere seven years after Debussy's death: Why had the academic world gone silent? Perhaps it was just a hoax — some overly sensitive Brit who objected so strongly to parallel unresolved dominant sevenths that he attempted to smear the perpetrator through a rag pamphlet. And that's what I felt increasingly over time as further study and research revealed no substantion of what had been implied in Harold's pamphlet. Until Paris, that is!

In the early '70s, I was in a small bookstore around the corner from the *Conservatoire de Paris* called *À La Flute de Pan* or Pan's Flute. There on a dusty shelf was a biography of Debussy in French. Inside, opposite the title page, was a photograph of Debussy that looked like this:

Underneath was a descriptive phrase indicating that Debussy himself had slashed the picture with a pair of scissors. A *frisson* shivered through my body and I nearly dropped the book.

Why? Why would Debussy gouge the image of his face like that? Was it a guilty conscience? Was it the tortured sickness of guilt for all those unmentionable heinous sins of the pamphlet that were too awful to discuss but everybody knew about?

By this time, I had studied not only Debussy's music in depth but had explored in detail the fascinating eccentricities of the *Fin du Siècle* period — the *L'Age D'Or* — as well as great pioneers of Modern Music like Schoenberg and Stravinsky. And while in a real sense Debussy was one of the major progenitors of modern music, there certainly were, from a purely musical point of view, wilder rule breakers, more odd eccentrics and more bizarre experimentalists who could have been hung, drawn and quartered on musical grounds for what they did. But there were no pamphlets about them and so scissor-slashed portraits.

So my quest continued fruitlessly. Nowhere could I find a hint, a reference that would lead me to an answer. Nothing. Nothing until 1983, when a friend recommended I read a fascinating book called *The Holy Blood and the Holy Grail.* In it, two populist authors investigate a secret society known as the Priory of Zion, or the *Prieurie de Sion* in French. Much of the book raises a lot of questions but rarely draws solid conclusions with sound evidence — perhaps largely because of the secret nature of this society.

However, in essence, here's the scoop:

1. Jesus and Mary Magdalene had a child.
2. Mary Magdalene brought the child, and the Holy Grail — the chalice from the Last Supper — to France.
3. Their line of descendants has continued down through the centuries, through Dagobert the Fourth, and whoever is head or President of the Priory of Zion is of that lineage. And that's a very succinct summary of hundreds of pages of details, references, questions and queries.

HOWEVER, there is a list of the Presidents of the Priory of Zion and I reprint itexactly as it occurs in the book:

Jean de Gisors	1188-1220
Marie de Saint-Clair	1220-66
Guillaume de Gisors	1266-1307
Èdouard de Bar	1307-36
Jeanne de Bar	1336-51
Jean de Saint-Clair	1351-66
Blanche d'Evreux	1366-98
Nicolas Flamel	1398-1418
René d'Anjou	1418-80
Iolande de Bar	1480-83
Sandro Filipepi	1483-1510
Léonard de Vinci	1510-19
Connétable de Bourbon	1519-27
Ferdinand de Gonzague	1527-75
Louis de Nevers	1575-95
Robert Fludd	1595-1637
Valentin Andrea	1637-54

Robert Boyle	1654-91
Isaac Newton	1691-1727
Charles Radclyffe	1727-46
Charles de Lorraine	1746-80
Maximilian de Lorraine	1780-1801
Charles Nodier	1801-44
Victor Hugo	1844-85
Claude Debussy	1885-1918
Jean Cocteau	1918-1963

And there you have it! Debussy was President of the Priory of Zion and therefore claimed to be a direct descendant of Jesus Christ and Mary Magdalene. The answer to my decades-old quest as to why the 1925 pamphlet was so vehement yet so obtuse. Although there are some FURTHER OBSERVATIONS:

1. How did somebody know about this back in 1925 ?
2. Why has academia, in countless biographic articles, essays and theses never even so much as hinted at or mentioned this fact?
3. Why are there censored portions of the diaries and letters etc. of Debussy?
4. Are there living relatives who are trying to protect themselves from media exposure if these stories were told?
5. Does the Priory of Zion still exist but have a power and influence sufficient to keep a pale of silence about its existence, its history and the shattering implication of its claims?

There are questions still to be answered!??"

With that, Colli picked up a hoarse chestnut that had fallen from the tree, cracked it open and rubbed it slowly in his left hand, pondering the grain and obviously appreciating the colour. It was one of the rarest moments of contemplative serenity I have ever observed the Maestro to indulge in. After a while, he stood up and wandered off past Scribbler's Silo across the asparagus patch and soon was lost to sight in the impenetrable darkness of Willurd's Woods.

And so, for this chapter, I leave you, dear reader, to wander off into your own woods and wonder about what you have just heard.

My next chapter involves fertilizer — and flying fertilizer at that — so bring towels and washcloths and we'll all be fine.

QUESTION: WHAT THE H_ _ _ HAPPENED CIRCA 1900?

"She's dried up!"

Those were the very words of Dr. Peter Blurgells, our Chezlee and environs veterinary Mother Theresa to the beasts. We'd called him after hours of yanking at those withered teats had produced not so much as a drop of Maude's bovine nectar. It was not long after she dried up, that she quietly passed on (as I mentioned in the Memoriam p.*). Sad that she no longer could provide for us, she just gave up.

Sorry, I got a bit overcome there; I was fond of the old cow. Just give me a minute and I'll recommence.

Continuing on, just like Maude's udder

MUSIC (kinda) DRIED UP

Composers of music were heard in their locals as they downed some absinthe or trinkletrocken or Stoney Ripples moaning statements like:

a) "Why bother trying? It's all been done before!" — Ennui de Bordom (Fr.)

2. "I've written the theme from the first movement of Beethoven's *Fifth Symphony* twice now. I didn't notice it till my cleaning lady pointed it out." — an honest composer.

iii) "We all have to do a little borrowing now and then" squirmed _ _ _ _ _ _ _ _ _ _ , at his lawyers' office, up on another plagiarism charge.

* Look it up yourself!

d) "I've been up and down and in and out of the major/minor scale till I'm blue in the face! There's no such thing as an original composition left. I'm going into dentistry! Or arc-welding." — a frustrated composer.

5. "We've got to find new ways to organize music! New sounds! New something. 'Cause the wine of creativity is bursting the seams of the old wine skins. Pour me another absinthe, waitress." — attributed to A. Scriabin.

vi) "As soon as I put down 1 bar of music I remember at least 50 songs that use exactly the same notes" — an anal-retentive, perfect-pitch perfectionist.

g) "I'm all dried up. I'm udderly exhausted." — attributed to Maude.

viii) "I've emoted my last passionate emote. I'm pooped out! I have no emotion left." — a defeated romantic.

So you see, that's what started happening circa 1900 (or just a bit after!).

Look at the world of the Visual Arts! (And I mean that lovingly!)

Look at Picasso! (And I mean that respectfully, as he was a genius!)

The man could draw magnificently. However, he too seemed to "dry up" (see Maude's udder) when around 1905, he painted the now-famous *Les Demoiselles D'Avignon* and blasted the blazes out of PERSPECTIVE — a concept that had been around for centuries.

Out of frustration came ABSTRACT PAINTING and CUBISM and whether you like it, or not, you've gotta sympathize with the poor bugger for simply saying "I've got to find a DIFFERENT WAY to paint 'cause it's already all been done before and I sure as HELL CAN DO IT, ... but ... there must be another way ..."

Now I'm *no* Picasso, but here's a pictorial representation of before and after.

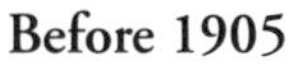

Before 1905

The same lady after 1905

Perhaps you can understand better if I tell you about the girdle Lucetta ordered from the catalogue. She'd picked out a lovely one with re-enforced steel girders in an aubergine shade and then looked at the size options: S M L XL. Unhappily, (this being her first catalogue girdle order) she mistakenly assumed these letters to stand for Super Moderate Light and Xtra Light, so she ordered the S.

LUCETTA: PRE-EXPLOSION!

The struggles we had following its delivery were gargantuan (as is Lucetta) and eventually, just as we were on the verge of closing the last clasp, the thing burst into a thousand smithereens, implanting steel and rubber bits in every pregnable surface, (and some impregnable ones!). One whizzing steel girder, powerfully propelled by "the flesh that could no long be contained" actually sliced off the lower left quadrant of the Maestro's beard and skewered his collection of Bach's *Well-Tempered Clavier* right up to *Fugue Number 22 in Bb minor*.

My point, you ask? Simply this: Lucetta's impressive girth could not be contained by the S-size mail-order catalogue foundation garment.

And, by comparison, MUSIC could no longer be restricted by the notes of the MAJOR and MINOR scales, measures with 2, 3 or 4 beats in them, and melodies that you could hum on your way home from the Friday Night Foxtrot-Box-Lunch Singles Do at the Church of the Nazarene Recreation Hall in the basement.

SOMETHING HAD TO BE DONE! SOMETHING AS POWERFUL AS PICASSO'S DECONSTRUCTION OF PERSPECTIVE AND REPRESENTATIONAL PAINTING AS IT HAD EXISTED FOR CENTURIES, NAY MILLENIA!

WHO BROKE THE FETTERS OF THE PAST AND BROUGHT US INTO THE MODERN MUSIC OF THE 20TH CENTURY? WHO?

Who indeed?

If your appetite has at all been whetted, turn to the next chapter for one of the answers.

But first ...

AN APPENDIX RE: THOSE DAMN DAMES OF AVIGNON (and what they did to ART and MUSIC!)

For no one, to the best of my knowledge, has dared to observe and state what I am about to. The Maestro has felt adamantly about this point for decades and has preached to everyone, from curator to cows, on the subject. As a matter of fact, he painted his own version of Picasso's *Les Demoiselle D'Avignon* on an old bleached tablecloth, hung it on the backside of the barn-slash-garage and used it as a dart board. I was never quite sure where the bullseye was but he must have hit it often for his constant shouts of "bullseye!" were heard down to the folks sitting outside Blender's Lawn Ornaments and Budgies Shop.

Here is a humble representation of same. The black dots are the dart-holes. Concentrations of dots would seem to indicate BULLSEYE areas altho' the logic escapes me:

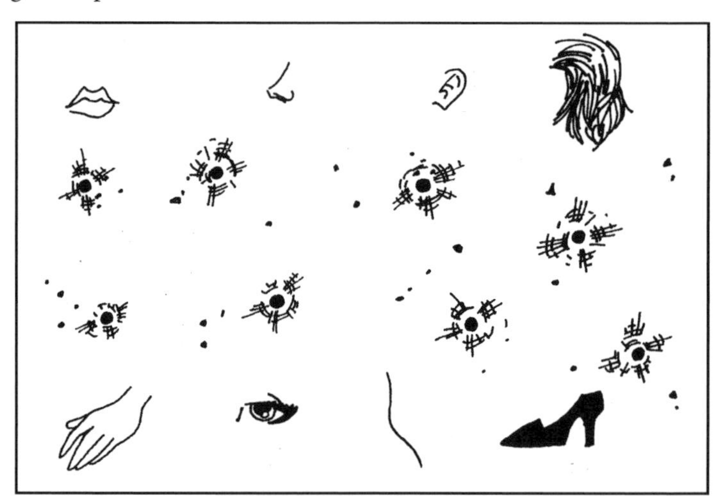

The Maestro's Dames of Avignon!!!

Now, let me hasten to assure the reader that Colli had the GREATEST RESPECT for Picasso and his genius. As a matter of fact, the Maestro had studied the works of Picasso, up to and including the ground-breaking *Demoiselle*, through each of Picasso's coloured periods and felt that he (Picasso) was one of the greatest craftsmen the art world had ever had.

However, having said all that, the Maestro would always say:

"Picasso CHOSE to paint the gals from Avignon like that so we 'have to' respect him for it, even though we're not quite sure why."

AND THAT'S WHEN IT HAPPENED! Colli would shout at the top of his voice. "What?" would respond the unsuspecting curate or cow that Colli was addressing. The answer would come in the same thundering capitals:

THE WHOLE WORLD FROM POPE TO PAUPER (AND PARTICULARLY THE GENERAL PUBLIC) ABDICATED THEIR RESPONSIBILITY TO

a) COMMENT ON
b) STATE THEIR OPINIONS
c) CRITIQUE OR QUESTION
d) GIVE THEIR PERSONAL REACTION TO ART!

A UNIVERSAL FEAR set in, whereby almost everybody was afraid to express their opinion about ART because the ARTIST just might be a GENIUS and had CHOSEN to produce that particular WORK OF ART so who the Hell are we to question him or her? We have played out, in the field of art, the EMPEROR'S NEW CLOTHES and have passed a century, fearful to say what we think or feel.

As a result of this abdication of our communal responsibility, we have suffered the following atrocities:

a) a MONKEY won a major painting competition in Chicago!

2) A MUSICAL PERFORMANCE lasts until at least 50% of the audience realizes that the players have no score, there is no score, and the musicians are just tooting, scraping and fooling around until most of the audience realize it is a hoax.

iii) flank steaks are arranged on a dressmaker's "judy" and hung in the National Art Gallery at great expense, but the "work of art" is removed after six weeks, due to the smell!

d) a clothesline is stretched diagonally from the top of one corner of a room to the bottom opposite corner, is called *Study in Diagonals* and costs a mint to buy.

The list goes on and on and on.

Now, DO NOT GET ME WRONG! The Maestro is no old fuddy-duddy conservative crank who says "Why can't things be the way they used to be?" NO!

He has studied the music of our century INTENSELY. He has written, himself, some of the most MODERN, EXPERIMENTAL, DARING WORKS I've ever heard. He is a PROGRESSIVE NON PAREIL.

BUT! He has always felt that art (and music) must NEVER EXIST IN ISOLATION or BE SEEN & HEARD ONLY BY THE ELITE. EVERYONE

SHOULD BE EXPOSED and EVERYONE should FEEL FREE to EXPRESS THEIR OPINIONS! Now, of course there's no need to be rude, but we also must exercise our democratic artistic rights in order to leaven the lump of Art and Music before it goes completely RANCID.

So his message is more of a CHALLENGE AND CALL TO
RE-ENTER THE FRAY
GET INTO THE RING
AND — NO MATTER WHO YOU ARE —
SAY WHAT YOU THINK ABOUT ART (including MUSIC).

Here's a list of thing you can do:

1. Go to art galleries, and if there's a book and a pen next to a Modern Art installation, for example, of gravel and sand in a wooden box separated by aluminium dividers, then pick up the pen and write your opinion in the book. For example: "This Installation 54210 is a pile of _ _ _ _."

2. Write the editor of your local newspaper (like the *Chezlee Sez*, for example) and tell them to fire the music critic whatever his or her name is, because he (or she) only reviews music that they have a CD of. This is fine for Beethoven or Mussorgski but is difficult for the première of NEW WORKS. Works that have been killed in their infancy by the harsh words of that _ _ _ _, whoever the critic is.

3. Put the role of music critic (and art in general) BACK IN THE HANDS OF THE PEOPLE, who are bloody well paying the $7.23 a seat (15% off for seniors and egg producers) and deserve to be heard.

4. If something looks like a "pile o'crap" or sounds like a "sow in heat," DO NOT BE AFRAID to say so. It well might be, given where ART and MUSIC are at nowadays. You should listen to it, give it a fair hearing and don't just dismiss it out of hand, but after that you're still entitled to say "Don't want to look at crap or hear pig's [dating], thank you very much."

In short, LOOK, LISTEN and SAY WHAT YOU THINK AND FEEL.

Artists, composers and people need to get re-connected!

CHAPTER 7:
THE FERTILIZER HITS THE FAN (12 TIMES)

I'd heard the expression thousands of times and imagined its unfortunate implications, but I am one of the few people to have actually experienced it.

It was a lovely sun-drenched summer's day, and I had just finished cleaning the stalls of Cliff and Clarice, our beloved bovines, and that of a guest nag we were tending while the McBrides were at a chicken-plucking convention in Dayton, Ohio. I had gathered a small pail of the combined bovine and equine droppings that I was intending to spread on the rutabagas and Savoy cabbage patch to aid in their growth, hoping for prizes in the Chezlee, Ont., Parsnips and Arts Fest Produce Contest.

Unbeknownst to me, Lucetta, eager for notice, if not first place, in the Original Art division of the same aforementioned Fest, had hand-painted an old sheet, tattered and limp with age, and was drying its fresh and sticky surface with a gi-normous fan that she'd borrowed from the abattoir. To set the scene, perhaps a picture will help, although I hasten to point out that painting was not Lucetta's *forte*.

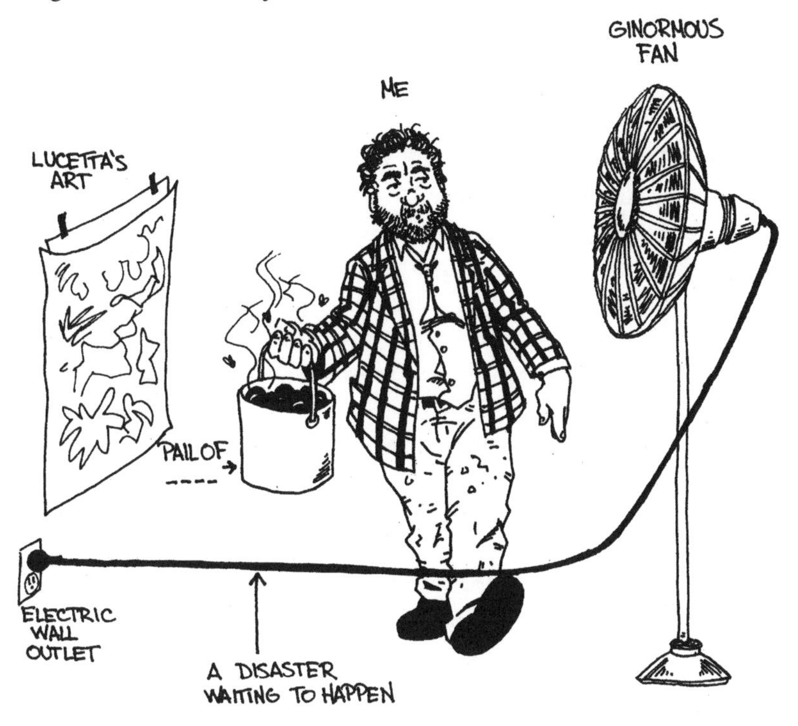

Needless to say, the following sequence of events occurred:

1. I tripped on the chord of the electric fan.
2. The pail flipped up and over.
3. Its contents fell in front of the powerful fan.
4. Its contents instantly were spread
   I) all over me
   ii) all over Lucetta's painted sheet
5. Somehow the fan remained plugged in.
6. I fled immediately to the pond, stripped, and tried to clean off the above-mentioned contents in its murky waters.
7. The fan, remaining on, dried hard that which had splattered on Lucetta's sheet-slash-*object d'art.*
8. Lucetta won first prize in the Original Art division of the Chezlee, Ont., Parsnips and Arts Fest for her work entitled *Patties in Pastures.**

Why relate such an unpleasant personal story? you may well ask.

But you know, dear reader, as in life, so in art. That's EXACTLY WHAT HAPPENED IN MUSIC and it wasn't_ _ _ _ , it was Schoenberg that hit the fan — 12 times, as a matter of fact.

Any discussion of music in the 20th century must contain some references to ARNOLD SCHOENBERG (1874-1951) mainly because of two reasons:

1. He broke completely with the tradition of music as it had existed from 1600-1900.
2. He invented a SYSTEM of composition that others could follow (like Freud did for psychiatrists).

Copious amounts have been written about this controversial composer, who, like Picasso, stands towering at the beginning of our century and music, like art, would never be the same after him. However, the purpose of my humble volume is not to write a history of 20th-century serious music, but

1. To nudge you, the reader-slash-listener to LISTEN to some Modern Music.
2. To bring to light certain aspects of the composers' lives and thoughts andconsequently their music that perhaps are overlooked or swept under the rug.
3. To expose the reader to the truth, and truths about what has happened to music in our century and that we'd better come to grips with it as we teeter on the verge of the next! (Century, that is)

A tidbit re: the life of Schoenberg:

a) He worked for a period of time IN A BANK.

b) He studied counterpoint with Alexander von Zemlinsky FOR A FEW MONTHS!

c) The above (b) was the ONLY MUSICAL INSTRUCTION HE EVER HAD!

d) He MARRIED ZEMLINSKY'S SISTER

Need I say more?

The people, I say, did not like Schoenberg's music and the feeling was mutual. Observe:

1. In 1900, several of his songs were performed at a concert in Vienna, and it PRECIPITATED A SCENE.

2. When Schoenberg's *Symphony Op. 9* was first performed, the audience WHISTLED and BANGED THEIR SEATS! (Those belonging to the hall, I mean!)

3. A friend said "We had sometimes to get Schoenberg out of the concert hall by a back entrance and had to shield him with our very own bodies against all the things that were surrounding him."

So what did Schoenberg do? Did he make his music easier to listen to, more accessible to the general public? Did he care? To find the answer to these (and other) questions, let's get it straight from the horse's mouth. Here are a series of direct quotes:

1. "If it is art, it is not for all, and if it is for all, IT IS NOT ART!"

2. "There are relatively few people who are capable of understanding, purely musically, what music has to say. Such trained listeners have probably never been very numerous, but that does not prevent the artist from creating only for them."

And if you think this sounds *un peu* snobbish, get a load of this anecdote:

In 1913, at the first performance of his *Gurreleide*, the audience absolutely loved it and responded with wild enthusiasm.Schoenberg was there and was called back time and again to acknowledge the audience's enthusiastic response. But what did he do, hmmm?

Schoenberg

1. bowed to, and thanked, the conductor.
2. bowed to, and thanked, the orchestra
3. BUT IGNORED THE OVATION OF THE PUBLIC

SCHOENBERG IGNORING THE PUBLIC

Furthermore, in speaking of the evening, he said: "For years those people who greeted me with cheers tonight refused to recognize me. WHY SHOULD I THANK THEM FOR RECOGNIZING ME NOW?"

And if you think that's arrogant, just listen to what he said when his *Violin Concerto Op. 36* was published in 1936:

"I am delighted to add another UNPLAYABLE work to the repertoire. I want the little finger to become LONGER. I CAN WAIT!"

Now, that's an attitude! We're talking Icarus, or Drabinsky, or watch out, Arnold, you could be cruisin for a fall!

But there you have it, straight from the composers' mouth, the basis of one of the problems of MODERN MUSIC in our century:

THE SPLIT BETWEEN

THE COMPOSER and THE PUBLIC

BOO!!
WE HATE YOU!
CRAP!
HISS!!

Schoenberg

Boo! Hiss! Tsk, tsk!

So Schoenberg, and many other serious composers of the 20th century hunkered down and IGNORED THE PUBLIC. He created in Vienna in 1918 The Society for Private Musical Performance. And there were Rules!

1. You had to be a MEMBER to get in.
2. Every work must be performed twice.

(This is actually a very good rule, as the first time you hear a "new" piece, it's difficult to absorb it all, so you need another run at it.I feel the same about dessert pies: I need a second piece, to assess their delicacies properly.)

3. All applause is forbidden.
4. All signs of disapproval — such as hisses, boos, raspberries, or tsks — are likewise forbidden.
5. NO CRITICS ALLOWED*

Schoenberg soon developed the following attitude:

I KNOW YOU HATE IT NOW, BUT

a) "In a few decades, audiences will recognize the TONALITY of this music today called ATONAL."

b) "ATONAL is what will be understood in the future."

c) "This is the essence of genius — IT IS IN THE FUTURE. This is why the genius is NOTHING TO THE PRESENT."

And thus Schoenberg gave birth to an ARTISTIC DICTUM that has governed the arts in general, and music specifically. And what is that ARTISTIC DICTUM? you ask. This:

SOUNDS LIKE _ _ _ _ !

OR

I KNOW IT LOOKS LIKE CRAP NOW!,

BUT

FUTURE GENERATIONS WILL CALL IT GREAT ART

Now, the Maestro has urgently requested a qualifying codicil, or rider, to the above DICTUM.

Qualifying Codicil:

Don't get me wrong!

b) I love, personally, much of Schoenberg's MUSIC.

c) I WANT YOU to listen to it and give his theory the test. Are you a "future generation" far away enough to love Schoenberg and consider its ATONALITY (formerly yukk!) Now TONAL (ooooh — that's lovely!)?

d) It's his ATTITUDE that bothers me.

e) And that this ATTITUDE has become a RULE FOR ALL ART IN THE 20TH CENTURY.

*I love this one — Would to God— also see my first book and the chapter called *Critis and the CLAP.*

I hope, dear reader, that you understand the points I'm making. I have the greatest respect for Schoenberg and his monumental contributions to music in our century (just as I have for Freud, although Jung (younger) and Adler (and others) carried his beginnings, further and deeper and better. And I'm not just saying that because Freud was tone deaf and based all his theories on upper-middle-class (already) neurotic Viennese women! (but that's another book)

BUT THERE ARE PROBLEMS. WITH THE ARTISTIC DICTUM of the 20th century (if you've forgotten it already, it's on the last page, for Pete's sake).

1. If it's only FUTURE GENERATIONS that will know what's GREAT ART, then WHY BOTHER LISTENING???

2. Monkeys can and do win 1st Prize in painting exhibitions and contests.

3. Curators of National Art Galleries pay a million bucks for FLANK STEAKS NAILED ON A DRESSMAKER'S JUDY

4 Performers improvise crap (burp, fart, twiddle, plunk, scrape and bang) and FOOL a bunch of composers and students gathered for a concert for 6½ minutes until the laughter of THE STUDENTS (and one in particular) caused the lead performer to say to the lighting man in the booth "Well that's it! It took longer than I expected!"

"Took longer to what?" you ask.

To realize that IT WAS ALL A HOAX.

Now, before I get off on another tangent, let us calmly return to the discussion at hand, which was ... which was ... oh yes ... Arnold Schoenberg and his contribution (which certainly was more than the $1.95 the Rev. MacDudd gave for the restoration of our historic Dodge-Desoto when it blew up after evensong in the church parking lot).

Now, I know that there is a question that is niggling many, if not all, of you — and the Maestro has just set me a stellar example by tackling the toughest task in Obscuria (the name we call our little home here in rural Chezlee, Ont.). He's taken saw, hammer, nails and boards and is heading up to the roof above the kitchen where Lucetta's pickling pot blew a hole through it when she added gasoline, instead of olive oil to her famous Lima Beans in Lard recipe.

As I was saying, the niggling question:

What did Schoenberg "invent" or "create" that was so earth-shatteringly controversial?

Well, I'm going to explain it to you. For those with respiratory ailments, irritable bowel syndrome or weak mathematical background, I would suggest you turn to p._ _ and skip this next bit, easy and accessible though it may be. (There's no test at the end, so you don't have to worry. Go have a cigarette and Stoney Ripple and join up with us on p._ _).

Here are the names used to describe Schoenberg's invention.

THE TWELVE-TONE SYSTEM
or DODECAPHONIC MUSIC
or SERIALISM
or (generally) ATONAL music,

"So???" and "That's no help at all" and "Weren't there always 12 tones in an octave?" I hear shouted from your ever-inquisitive minds. Well, that's true but it's all in how you use them.

HITHERTO

Music was based on the Major/Minor scale or TONALITY but there was a hierarchical way of using them.

For example, let's look at the scale of C major on the keyboard:

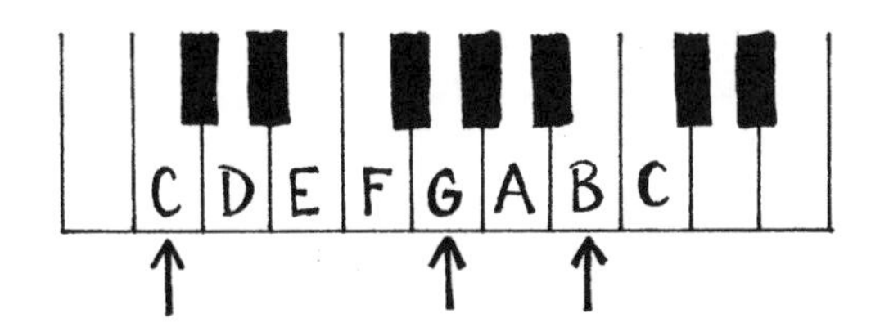

above the white keys are black keys or notes, used sometimes, but definitely in a lower class than the scale itself

The first note is C, the note the scale is named after. It's call the TONIC, it's where you start from and end up, it's home! It's the most important note in the scale.

G is called the DOMINANT and judging from some of the ads I've seen in the back pages of the *Chezlee Sun* about Domination, this is a very powerful note that has tremendous control.

B is the LEADING NOTE and while it has a certain strength, it's main function is to LEAD US next door to the UPPER TONIC (C). It's sort of a royal page whose job is to say "Here comes the Tonic."

Harmonies are built on combinations of notes called TRIADS — 3 of every other note.

In C major, the three most importantTRIADS are:

G E C	C A F	D B G
The Tonic or I	The Sub- Dominant or IV	The Dominant or V

So you see, it's a hierarchical structure involving Kings, Queens, subjects and peasants.

Powerful notes, important notes, not-so-important notes, and downright throwaways. And that's the way music was for centuries.

HOWEVER, SCHOENBERG said (and here I fantasize):

"This system is pooped out. You can't possibly write anything new. It's all been written before. We need a NEW SYSTEM!" So he invented the 12-TONE MUSIC or SERIALISM

It was like the French or American Revolution, for he said:

1. ALL TONES ARE EQUAL (all 12 of them)
2. SELECT YOUR OWN SERIES OF 12 TONES
3. This is the new scale or (as he called it) TONE ROW or (for short) ROW upon which you base your piece of music.
4. You can use this ROW in 4 ways:

a) AS IT IS
b) INVERTED (fancy word for upside-down)
c) RETROGRADE (fancier word for backwards)
d) RETROGRADE INVERSION (even fancier word for backwards and upside-down)

Here's an example of a basic ROW

1 8 12 9 6
2 10 5 4 11 7 3

MUSICAL (or at least TONAL) DEMOCRACY HAD BEEN DECLARED!

The last thing I want to say about Schoenberg is not more pedantic analysis but a few words about the OVERALL EFFECT OF SCHOENBERG'S MUSIC

1. "furious restlessness"
2. "well-nigh hysterical emotionality"
3. unresolved dissonance
4. order does not triumph over chaos
5. The score — to *look* at — is the epitome of logic, order, control and discipline

BUT

The score — to *LISTEN* to — is the epitome of random, aimless, arbitrary, whimsical, angst-filled wanderings

6. Schoenberg himself said "I write what I feel in my heart — and what finally comes on paper is what first coursed through every fibre of my body. A work of art can ... achieve no finer effect than when it transmits to the beholder the emotions that ... raged in the water, in such a way that they rage and storm also in him."
7. "maximum intensity at all times."

Now, this last point (no. 7) reminds me of that fervent and fanatical pastor of the Chezlee, Ont., Church of the Almighty (Independent), who functions at maximum intensity all the time, and frankly, I can only take about three minutes max of the chap before I want to strangle him.

Similarly, with the music of Schoenberg:

1. Don't put it on as background music for a quiet dinner with friends.
2. Don't play it in the car whilst driving. CAA & insurance companies explicitly do not handle what could result consequentially.
3. Have an antacid on hand!
4. It's an IDEAL Christmas gift for an annoying in-law and a note saying "Thinking of you at this season."

But above all

Remember:

LISTEN TO SOME SCHOENBERG

LISTEN TO IT TWICE

DO IT PRIVATELY AND QUIETLY IN THE CONTEXT OF YOUR OWN SPACE.

Use Schoenberg as that "toe in the water" of the sea of music of the 20th century.

It's amazing how quickly you'll warm to it and many other composers that you have hereunto simply and immediately written off. So step into the sea of Modern Music and wait for that "take your breath away" time when the waters of music hit the naughty bits.

And remember what one of Schoenberg's student said:

"After all, a masterpiece is in no hurry. It transcends time. It can be misunderstood or ignored — all this is quite unimportant and the time will come when its beauty will be revealed WITHOUT ANY OUTSIDE ASSISTANCE."*

*Although, almost a century later, I'm having to write this damn book to try to help assist you, dear reader!

CHAPTER 8:

THE NIGHT THEY RIPPED THE SEATS OUT AT THE FOUR SQUARE GOSPEL HALL

BETTY (one of the sturdy Sappho Singers)
CAUGHT STEALING ONE OF THE RIPPED OUT
SEATS FROM THE 4 SQUARE G.H.

Maestro Colli Albani, as I'm sure you have garnered, dear reader, is a man above other men in learning, insight, forthrightness and furrowing (he's won the Finest Furrower First Prize twice, over the years — and there are no other musicologists who even bothered entering the contest).

However, it's a little-known fact that, in his youth, he was also, among all of his other monumental accomplishments, an innovative, *avant-garde*, nay even radical composer. I'll never forget the night he premiered his early work, albeit experimental, called:

Hog Calls and Hens In Heat:
An instrumental and choral fantasy
scored for
2 flutes (for the première there was only one, as Bythinia got cramps)
5 trombones (from the Junior Boys Spelunking Marching Band)
1 sow (Irene — the McNullought's)
2 overturned washtubs (ours!)
3 hens (the O'Rority's)
2 police whistles (stolen)
1 pail of lard (which never got used due to what happened)

A female chorus (the Maestro hired the Sappho Singers from down Desborough way — a husky bunch of "girls" whose bottoms went as low as B-flat)

To describe what happened that unforgettable night as the Maestro's baton came down at 8:07 p.m. (They had to wait for trombone No. 4 as the Men's was out of order and he had to use the Ladies' and scared Euphemia half to death) would require a book in itself.

At this time, the ladies (and Percival) of the Central Committee of the Chezlee Parsnip and Arts Fest were just beginning their laudable efforts to expose the listening public of Chezlee, Ont., to the challenges of Modern Music. It was one of their first exposures, however, and, as a result, some burning did occur.

None of us, however, was prepared for what happened during the third movement called: *THE MATING TARANTELLA (molto libido)*

This boisterous and explorative movement had just gotten off to a vigorous start when the closest thing to ALL HELL BREAKING LOOSE occurred and turned the Four Square Gospel Hall into a state of chaos. Let me just say that it involved Irene (the sow), seven of the sturdy Sappho Singers from down Desborough way, 2 trombonists, Emmett and Eugene, and 2 of the McNullought's hens. I would not dare do a pictorial representation of this calamitous event, but would simply record that by the time Constable Crump and Wilf Waldmire, his voluntary assistant, had cleared the crowd out ALL THE SEATS AT THE F.S.G.H. HAD BEEN RIPPED OUT!!!

What better way to introduce the composer whose contribution to the birth of, the midwife of, nay the production of, much Modern Music?

I speak of course of IGOR STRAVINSKY (1882-1971).

Stravinsky, or rather his music, is probably, or possibly more familiar to the listening public than many of the other modern composers that have been or will be, dealt with in my modest tome. Be that as it may, there are nuggets here, gems, a "turn of phrase" and a few facts (albeit reminders) that it would be meritorious to revisit at this juncture. And so, being a man of few words, let's to'it!

The music of Stravinsky can be divided into 3 periods:

1. WILD
2. ORDERED AND DISCIPLINED
3. BIT O'THIS, BIT O'THAT

and we will discuss him (and it) in that order.

1. Stravinsky's WILD PERIOD

Now, we've all had them, dear reader, so don't be too quick to pass judgement. I'm sure there are a few early irregularities in each and every one of your lives that you wouldn't want bruited about. I know there are in mine.

Nasty insinuations and sinister suggestions have been made occasionally in the *Chezlee Sez* as to certain "departures from the norm" in both the Maestro's and my juvenile past but I assure the reader, if he or she has read and wondered, they are purely speculative and both Colli and I have kept our wild bits very private.

Unfortunately, Stravinsky's wild bits were publicly performed, subsequently published (both the score and the furour) and therefore available for all the world to see and, in his case, hear.

Russian born (in Oranienbaum — Isn't that a lovely sounding name? Say it five times It should be set to music) and trained, he somehow hooked up with, at a very early age, (28) the legendary impressario of the *Ballets Russe* (or, in English, the Russian Ballet), Serge Diaghilev.

He wrote the music for the company's 1910 production, *L'Oiseau de Feu* (or *The Firebird*). This was such a hit, he was hired the next year to write *Petrushka* and in 1913, wrote the famous (or infamous) *Le Sacre du Printemps* or *The Rite of Spring*.

Now, if you can remember that far back, I started this chapter with a lurid description of "the night they tore the seats outa' the Four Square Gospel Hall."

Tho' that night in Chezlee, Ont. was a bit later than 1913, that's EXACTLY WHAT HAPPENED in Paris the night they premiered *The Rite of Spring*. Talk about a riot! One contemporary account tells of an audience member whose head was used as a tom-tom by the violent pounding of the gentleman standing up behind him in the next row. (And I must say, that as wild as things have ever gotten at the good ol' Four Square, there has NEVER BEEN VIOLENT HEAD THUMPING & THWACKING!)

"Why? Why? Why?" I hear echoing through the empty corridors of my mind from you, dear readers. So, timidly but with forthrightness, I will answer your queries and, in my typical logical and ordered fashion, will lay it out for you clearly and numerically, so's you'll understand

WHY DID *THE RITE OF SPRING* CAUSE A RIOT?

1. Subject Matter — in general it's described as SCENES OF PAGAN RUSSIA, but just look at some of the titles of certain sections, and descriptions thereof:

ADORATION OF THE EARTH, DANCE OF THE ADOLESCENTS, GAME OF ABDUCTION (youths and maidens from phalanxes approach and withdraw from one another; they perform the Dance of the Earth) THE SACRIFICE — *a sacrificial maid must be chosen to ensure the Earth's fertility MYSTIC CIRCLE OF YOUNG GIRLS THE DANCE IN ADORATION OF THE CHOSEN VIRGIN (frenzied) RITUAL ACT OF THE OLD MEN — "swaying bodies and shuffling feet"* SACRIFICIAL DANCE OF THE CHOSEN MAIDEN — *(she dances till she falls dead and the men in wild excitement bear her body to the foot of the mound of earth)*

Need I say more? This is no musical setting of *Goldilocks* or *Cinderella*! Talk about a "GRIMM" tale! What with old men, young virgins, frenzied dancing, swaying bodies and shuffling feet, the only thing it puts me in mind of is Old Queenie's Café and Grill down the 9th Concession on the outskirts of Feverville and the rumours that have circulated about her place for years!

However, point 1 has taken up a whole page and we haven't even hit the music yet! No wonder they ripped out their seats!

2. The Music — here are some descriptions:

— revolutionary
— strong dissonance
— high dissonance
— low dissonance
— dissonance everywhere
— a violent style
— the bar line was eliminated!
— POUNDING rhythms
— BOLD harmonies
— BITONALITY (2 keys at a time!)

Now, I could go further, but I don't want to get too technical here because my motive is

1. NOT TO ANALYSE AND DISSECT TO DEATH
2. BUT TO TANTALIZE
TEASE
EVOKE a response
PROVIDE a little pinch on your musical behind to get you to
BUY THE CD and a good SINGLE-MALT SCOTCH
and
LISTEN TO THE DAMN THING.

Why not organize a *Rite of Spring* Party?

a) invite friends (preferably married couples in long-standing stable relationships)

b) serve drinks (Scotch or beer but no "coolers") and

c) have a GROUP LISTEN to *The Rite of Spring.*

This finishes the WILD PERIOD. We now move on to discipline!

Stravinksy's SECOND PERIOD: DISCIPLINE & ORDER

Now, first off, I know what some of your "*double entendre*" folk are thinking and that's not what I mean! (Although strangely enough, it does apply to the Australian/English composer/arranger Percy/Grainger. Whoops! That was one too many slashes — although Percy did enjoy it and the musical proof lies in his famous arrangement of *In an English Country Garden*).*

No! Stravinsky had a kind of conversion after his WILD PERIOD and there are, the Maestro and I feel, very strongly,

3 REASONS for Stravinsky's conversion from WILD to DISCIPLINED:

a) World War I — the general horror and devastation of it all, but especially the fact that it wiped out a lot of manpower, specifically orchestra players. After 1918, there wasn't a complete symphony orchestra left in Europe.

b) the Bolshevik Revolution in his beloved homeland and the establishment of communism in government. This virtually expelled him from his country for life!

c) Stravinsky had had ENOUGH OF WAGNER

Although music was already two decades into the new century and Wagner had died in 1883, which was 35 years before 1918, the spectre of Wagner's musical ghost STILL LOOMED LARGE! In the late 19th century he was worshipped as some kind of God-Man and his death (sorry, no ressurection) brought even more *post-mortem* adulation and Stravinsky HAD HAD ENOUGH! Listen to what he says about Wagner's book on *Music & Drama* and his resultant operas:

— "A TERRIBLE BLOW UPON MUSIC ITSELF or

— "The Art-Religion, with its HEROIC HARDWARE, its ARSENAL OF WARRIOR MYSTICISM and its vocabulary seasoned with an ADULTERATED RELIGIOSITY." (There's a bit of anti-German WWI sentiment here, but you do get the picture he didn't like Wagner, or what he thought, or what he composed.) or

— Stravinsky talks about his distaste for "HOLLOW TWADDLE AND BOMBAST, FALSE PATHOS AND LACK OF DISCRETION IN CREATIVE EFFUSION!"

May I interject a personal note at this juncture and say to you, Irvin Tornquist, so-called Music Critic of the *Chezlee Sez*, that I thought there was a familiar ring to this last quote of Stravinsky about Wagner's music, so I looked through some past issues and discovered that that's EXACTLY WHAT

*Look at it sometime! As it builds to a thundering climax look at the *ffff*'s, the "with the fist" or "with the hand, wrist and forearm up to the elbow!" Discipline or being disciplined was a fondness of Percy's but that is NOT what we're talking about here!

YOU WROTE about the première of a combined Darling/Albani composition called *Phantom Phantasy on Phyllis Pharmer's Phyllidandrums*.

An experimental work, albeit, but for you to steal lines from Stravinsky — Irvin, have you no morals as well as no taste?

Anyway, to get back on the track now that I've got that out of my craw, we have discussed the three reasons for Stravinsky's conversion from WILD to DISCIPLINED but we need to hear from the man himself, and let's start off with his dictum!

Stravinsky's Dictum:

RHYTHM AND MOTION (NOT FEELING) ARE THE FOUNDATIONS OF MUSICAL ART.

Now, you must remember, avid observer, that MUSIC had just gone through almost 100 years of the ROMANTIC PERIOD and I'm sure that you will agree that after a romantic period of a hundred years, your

a) feelings would be pooped out
b) you'd want a cigarette for sure
c) it would be nice to do something else for a while like
  i) a cryptic crossword
  ii) a walk in the park to feed the ducks
  iii) check out the stock market

So, you see, it's no wonder that Stravinsky said — and this is not a direct quote:

ENOUGH OF FEELING ALREADY! LET'S JUST LISTEN TO THE MUSIC ITSELF!

Now for the words from the horse's (Stravinsky's) mouth.

1. "The more RESTRICTIONS I impose on myself the more my mind is LIBERATED FROM ITS SHACKLES."

2. "I cannot compose until I have decided what PROBLEM I must SOLVE."

3. "Music is powerless to EXPRESS anything that is NOT ITS PURPOSE. There is an emotion aroused by Art, but it is DIFFERENT."

4. "I evoke neither human joy nor human sadness, I move towards an even greater ABSTRACTION."

Now do you get the picture? These quotes are admittedly a bit extreme, and, in actual fact, most people do get quite an EMOTIONAL WHALLOP even from Stravinsky's most disciplined and abstract works. But it shows the direction he was taking.

There are two names for this "between the wars" period of 1918-1939, and a lot of composers, besides Stranvinsky, felt that they needed a bit of DISCIPLINE and ORDER in their lives.

This "*inter-bellum*" period was called

A. Back to Bach

or B. Neo-Classicism

NEO-CLASSICISTS DRAW ON THE OLD MASTERS

Both of them are wrong, says the Maestro, and Stravinsky himself disliked the term neo-classicism, but they reflect a changed attitude toward the purpose of music.

Colli has just popped in, looking for the pinking shears to trim the Ivy Lace Vine over the hen house, as the roosters' accessibility to the hens has been severely hampered. He has suggested a "list of clarification" about this *inter-bellum* attitude in my own words.Great genius that he is, he recognizes the importance of succinct simplicity. So here goes:

NEO-CLASSICISM (in my own words):

1. Music is neither a God nor a religion.

2. Music ain't about pictures, books, stories, dreams, visions, ethics, morality, etc.

3. Music is about MUSIC.

4. Even tho' the un-trained or un-tutored and technically non-cognizant can listen to 20th-century neo-classical music and "feel" some kind of "emotion" from listening to it, THAT'S NOT WHAT IT'S ABOUT!

At this point, I feel there have been far too many WORDS about Stravinsky and we need a LIST of WHAT TO LISTEN TO from the DISCIPLINE & ORDER PERIOD:

1918 *L'Histoire d'un Soldat* (*A Soldier's Story*) — a musical drama for 3 characters, 1narrator and 7 instruments. (Look at the date and think!)

1918 *Ragtime for Eleven Instruments* — he'd heard of Scott Joplin?

1919 *Pulcinella* — a ballet for voice and SMALL orchestra. (Picasso did set and costumes! — WOW!)

1920 *Symphony of Wind Instruments* — dedicated to Debussy's memory (Note: Colli and I tried a similar experiment in 1973 with *Bagpipes, Balloons, Garden Hoses, Kazoos and Hot Water Bottles*. It was NOT well received by the general public and the music critic of the *Chezlee Sez*, Irvin Tornquist, was rude and vulgar in his condemnation of our effort. Still, even I have to admit, I do prefer Stravinsky's *Winds* to our own.)

1922 *Le Renard* (The Fox) — a "burlesque Tale" (Makes you wonder ...? — take a listen)

1923 *Les Noces* (*The Wedding*) — for 4 singers plus chorus, dancers and 4 (FOUR!) pianos.

1927 *Oedipus Rex* — an "opera-oratorio." The text (in Latin) is a translation of JEAN COCTEAU'S French adaptation of the Greek tragedy. And if you're not multi-lingually challenged by now, let me further blow your mind by this:

Jean Cocteau was, like Debussy, a President of the Priory of Zion, from 1918 (the year Debussy died) — and I'll leave that there, although I notice that the book *The Holy Blood and The Holy Grail* is referred to, in a yellow strip across the cover, as "THE EXPLOSIVELY CONTROVERSIAL INTERNATIONAL BESTSELLER"

1930 *SYMPHONY OF PSALMS*

I only have one thing to say: GO AND LISTEN TO IT!

THEN, if you dare, come back and tell me that you still hate Modern Music. Now, if it's your virginal excursion into Modern Music, be gentle — don't turn the volume up too high. And, after first hearing, have a Craven A and glass of white wine (dry, preferably) and do it again — I mean listen to it again!

I'M SURE YOU'LL LOVE IT!

Remember: These are just a few samplings! Although the guy was vertically challenged he churned out a ton of music over a long period of time. So it's a MULTIPLE CHOICE question when it comes to "What'll I listen to by Stravinsky?"

Finally,

C. Or 3. or iii) Stravinsky's THIRD PERIOD:

BIT O'THIS, BIT O'THAT

Let me state, right now, that Stravinsky (like Colli and I) has his CRITICS. And one of the main reasons he's criticized is that you can't pin him down, you can't categorize him, you can't put him in one pidgeonhole and leave him there.

He changed! And according to "the critics," this is WRONG.

Well, I say, BULLROAR! That's the same kinda crap we get hurled at us by Irvin Tornquist.

"We're growing!"

"We're changing!"

"We're developing!"

"We're tryin' somethin' NEW!"

We continue in vain.

And that's what Stravinsky did in his third period. He even tried SERIALISM! (Remember, I don't mean watching soaps like *As the Gut Reacts* or a diet of oats and bran, which can be messy!) I mean 12-tone music *à la* Schoenberg.

I could at this juncture give you another list of what to listen to of Stravinksy's Third Period but I shan't, for two reasons:

1. Colli has just yelled loudly, having read over my shoulder:"DON'T MOLLYCODDLE THEM! MAKE THEM GO OUT AND SEARCH.It's good for the musical soul as well as the fallen arches to encourage them to do a bit of digging for themselves!"

2. It's laundry night and Lucetta has demanded my complete wardrobe, leaving me the alternatives of the weekend paper or a bedsheet, so I'm opting for the latter and going to bed and, I want to start a new chapter in the morning so that's it for Stravinsky.

Truly, he's one of the GREATEST of our century so give him a LISTEN! (Stravinsky, I mean.)

Night!

A SEEMINGLY UNRELATED DIVERSION (which isn't)
or
THE BOSWELL/JOHNSON INTERCHANGE AND ITS MODERN RELEVANCE

Recently, the Maestro, Lucetta and I took a brief break from our strenuous musicological-slash-domestic-slash-agricultural duties (ranging in breadth from fugal analysis to asparagus-stalk shredding) and passed a pleasant weekend away in neighbouring Bunions' Corners (named after Captain B.B. Bunion, who, as well as commanding a small boat on Crabbe Lake, had invented head cheese). Though only 13 kilometres from Chezlee, Ont., it seemed as if we were miles away in some exotic, foreign oasis.

Whilst there, we happened to be sauntering through the Bunions' Corners Milk Can and Butter Churn Museum when I made a most AMAZING DISCOVERY. Hidden at the bottom of a dusty, cobwebbed churn was a copy, published in 1798, of *Dr. Johnson's Table Talk, Containing Aphorisms on Literature, Life and Manners with Anecdotes of Distinguished Persons, selected and arranged from Mr. Boswell's Life of Johnson.*

By the time I'd read the title, the museum had closed. Fortunately, Lucetta and the Maestro heard my cries and helped me out through the lavatory window. My hands were still trembling with anticipatory delight as, later, I opened the precious treasure in the Bunions' Corners Bide-a-Bit motel, and I was not disappointed.

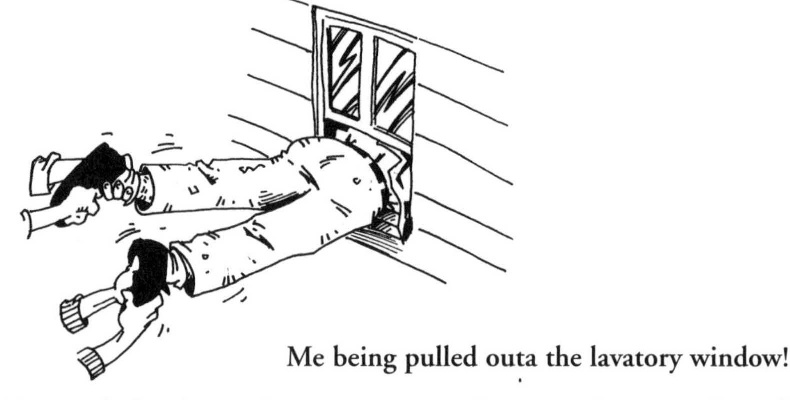

Me being pulled outa the lavatory window!

However, before sharing the nuggets I garnered, I must inform you of a small technological problem regarding printing and publishing in 1798. For some reason, and for some time, at this time SOME (but not all) letter S's were represented by something that looks like the letter F. For example, instead of Susie Smith, you would have Fusie Fmith.

Now, as awkward and difficult as it is, I feel duty-bound by my respect for the past to present any quotes from the book exactly as they appear in it! And now to share with you my exciting and relevant discoveries, which, to print it in Boswellian terms, are fimply ftupendouf:

1. Discovery Number one:

Once, while attending a musical party, Dr. Johnson confessed to Boswell that he was "very infenfible to the power of mufick."

Boswell responded by saying that music affected him to a great degree, agitating his nerves painfully and producing in his mind "alternate fenfations of pathetic dejection, fo that I was ready to fhed tears; and of daring refolution, fo that I was inclined to rufh into the thickeft part of the battle."

In reply, Johnson tersely retorted:

"Fir, I fhould never hear it, if it made me FUCH A FOOL!"

Try, dear reader, to calm yourself from the sheer power of this shocking revelation. How well he knew the seductive force of the sirens of music and its ability to induce all sorts of behavioural responses. Now, Boswell (and Johnson) were discussing their reactions to a delightfully innocent bit of 18th-century fluff called *Let Ambition Fire thy Mind*. How much more applicable is Johnson's pithy retort to the music of our own cenutry? How often has the incredible breath of sounds, generally described as Modern Music made us, dear reader and fellow listener, want to "FUCH A FOOL!?"

2. The Second Discovery

The following interchange I will simply quote directly as it occurs in the tex, and then we'll wallow in its implications:

A GENTLEMAN: "There is no beauty in a fimple find, but only in a harmonious compofition of founds."

BOSWELL: (Differing from this position, mentions "the foft and fweet found of a fine woman's voice")

JOHNSON: "No, Sir, if ferpent or toad uttered you would think it ugly."

ALL: "Ha, Ha, Ha, Ha, Ha." (laughing)

And there you have it! In 1798! A glimpse of one of the most radical innovations of the 20th century, that ALL SOUNDS are GRIST FOR THE MILL OF MUSIC.

Why, I myself once wrote a *Passacaglia* for a chorus of bullfrogs, Chinese temple gongs and two piccoli to be performed down at the Scribbler's Swamp on a warm summer evening after dark. And, as you have read, or will read, this was a tenet of that radical experimentalist JOHN CAGE, whose explorations of all sounds have become world renowned. Yet there you have it, tucked away in a two-page essay on MUFICK in Dr. Johson's *Table Talk* in 1798.

The nuggets are there, dear friend, if you are willing to pan through the butter churns of learning, sift through the detritus of time and discover them.

Let's allhave a round of Stoney Ripple to toast our discoveries, recover from the shock of it all and a second round as we sing a chorus of *Make me fuch a fool.*

CHAPTER 11:
ELLROY FRUMPPE'S SHOCKING CONTRIBUTION

Hitherto the names of Benjamin Franklin and Thomas Edison have been associated with the discovery of and development of electricity. But I'm prepared to wager a not-insignificant amount that very few of you have ever heard of our local pioneer in the electronic movement — namely, Ellroy Frumppe. This being the case, I feel that a short history would be in order at this junction.

Ellroy Frumppe was born in the latter days of the 19th century. The family were from Squiggin's Township, down the 4th Concession Line, and were into pigs, mostly. Ellroy married the young and lovely Wilda Walmsley and they settled down to continue his family's traditional occupation — namely, pigs. To that end, Ellroy had one of the largest silos in the Chezlee, Ont., environs and certainly the tallest. The significance of this becomes evident the night of the Great Storm of '25!

The devastation wrought by wind, rain and lightning that nasty night has been well recorded in the historical annals of Chezlee, Ont., so I won't delve further there but focus instead on Ellroy.

In the midst of that great storm, Wilda noticed that loosened bricks from the top of their silo were being hurled towards their cozy home and had already shattered three windows and knocked Persephone, their cat, totally cross-eyed and semi-conscious.

"You've got to fix it!" yelled Wilda above the thunderous din and howling winds. And as it was Wilda who "wore the overalls," so to speak, in their domestic arrangement, Ellroy did.

Well, to cut a long story a bit shorter, as Ellroy was up-silo fixin' bricks, needless to say — LIGHTNING STRUCK.

Ellroy Frumppe lighting up a bulb

The strangest miracle of all was that Ellroy was NOT killed on the spot. Nevertheless, there were ramifications. Somehow the monumental electric force passed through his light frame, down through the silo and lit the silage contained therein with such force that it blew Ellroy clear across county. He was found, three days later, still alive, but hanging from the spire of Twitchtoun's Roman Catholic Church — St. Systemia's of the Black-Eyed Susans.

Though shaken, Ellroy seemed to all outward observations perfectly fine and it wasn't until a few days later that his wife Wilda made the first amazing discovery.

Something had gone wrong with their old Marconi radio set and Wilda being the mechanic of the family had taken to "fixin' the damn thing." In the process of which, at one point, she threw the plug to Ellroy to hold while she "fiddled with the wall socket."

Suddenly the room was filled with the sounds of a foreign language (later discovered to be Laplandish). Upon experimentation they discovered that if Ellroy held the plug in his hand, they could receive not only CKWHY, the local Chezlee, Ont., radio station, but also radio bands from around the world. (They particularly enjoyed the Bavarian Oom-pah-pah Band Program from Klassenstrasse in Austria on Thursday nights at 10 p.m.)

Ellroy, it seems, had become an ELECTRONIC TRANSFORMER. However, there were pros and cons *vis-à-vis* his "shocking" disposition. Namely:

ADVANTAGES:

1. Ellroy could toast a slice between his knees.
2. He could heat water with his big toe (left).
3. He was a permanent lightning rod that protected the area when they placed him out in the open field behind the abattoir.
4. His hair was permanently curly. This is significant.
5. When he sang, it was a PURE ELECTRONIC SOUND!

DISADVANTAGES:

1. He and Wilda had 37 children until Wilda said "That's enough" and they got twin beds.
2. There was a certain "halo" of light surrounding him that scared the daylights out of small children, visiting governmental bureaucrats and the odd tourists that came to see him. (Tho' scaring off government bureaucrats isn't such a bad thing, really.)
3. Both the Pentecostals and the Catholics claimed him as a saint-slash-prophet because of his "sign and wonders" and got into terrible inter-ecclesiastical disputes about it, which caused the O'Raritys to move

down to Keadleigh and the Pattersnipes to leave the Pentecosts and open a Smoke Shop & Pool Hall in S'merdferd.

With reference to ADVANTAGES No. 5 — namely, Ellroy's singing — he became somewhat of a local phenomenon and as early as the early '30s an extremely young burgeoning musical *savant* by the name of Colli Albani (not yet a Maestro) was writing *avant-garde* songs for Ellroy to sing with his PURE ELECTRONIC SOUND voice.

These early experiments, however, sadly, failed as the visual appeal of poor Ellroy sitting on the stage reading Colli's complex scores was limited. And as Ellroy was unable to form words when he sang, it was a little too purely musical for the local concert goers. He did, however, manage a nice side-career with the midway of a travelling circus based in Wilkerstown and, apart from a brief affair with a bearded lady (who, it turns out, wasn't) had a pretty good time.

All this, however, is merely to introduce the phenomena of the 20th century that technical advances allowed — namely, ELECTRONIC MUSIC.

When we look at ELECTRONIC MUSIC beyond the unique contribution of Ellroy Frumppe in the Chezlee, Ont., area — i.e. the broader picture — there are

TWO IMPORTANT INVENTIONS upon which electronic music is based.

1. An "instrument" (machine) that produces purely electronic sounds, and
2. The TAPE RECORDER.

In today's world, honestly now, I ask you, who is not familiar with

a) synthesizers

or doesn't

b) own a small (or large) tape recorder?

These two great inventions of our century have come into the hands of virtually any and every Tom, Dick or Harriet.

All one has to do is attend a contemporary film (usually B-grade or further along the alphabet) and listen to the boring, monotonous, highly repetitious electronically (synthesizer) produced score to hear the application of these two inventions in today's everyday world.

However, let us look at how these electronic advances influenced the world of serious music and discuss some of the problems (and there were some). Essentially, there have been Three Schools of Electronic Music.

First School — The French — *MUSIQUE CONCRÈTE*

Right off the bat, let me tell you that this is not music based on the sound of concrete being mixed, poured or just sitting there on a pavement.

Colli and I made that mistake early on in our careers, and the trouble we got into when we hired old man Eeble's Cement Mixer, got it into the Four Square Gospel Hall and it spilled was difficult to live down.

Musique Concrète means taping sounds from non-musical sources and manipulating them electronically. Here's a list of possible sounds:

1. chickens
2. car horns in traffic jams
3. paint drying
4. a blazing fire
5. a tin can factory
6. ... what have you

Put these sounds on tape, then combine them, play them fast and/or slow, forwards and/or backwards, etc. etc. and you end up with *musique concrète.*

Three important names of this French School whom you should go out, buy a CD and listen to are:

1. Edgar Varèse (early)
2. Pierre Scheaffer
3. Pierre Boulez and also
4. Olivier Messiaen.

If you're just starting out in this field, a good "training bra" work to listen to would be Boulez's *Le Marteau sans Maître* (*The Hammer without a Master*).

Second School — The American

These guys take sounds from traditional musical instruments and the human voice (not Ellroy Frumppe's) and transform them electronically. The pioneers are:

1. Otto Luening
2. Vladamir Ussachusky
3. Roger Sessions
4. Milton Babbitt

Third School — The German

Karlheinz Stockhausen is the leading composer of this electronic gang and there are RULES.

Rule Number One: Electronic Music is a term that can only be applied to music using PURELY ELECTRONICALLY PRODUCED SOUNDS.

Rule Number Two: Following on from Schoenberg and his pupil Webern, they use the 12-Tone system or SERIALIZATION but apply it to all aspects, including rhythm, dynamics, timbre and density, resulting in TOTAL CONTROL.

Personal comment: Freud would probably have a field day analyzing these Germans and their need for total control. However, like Schoenberg's music, in spite of all the intricate complex mathematic structural control on the graph paper, the overall effect is whimsical fluff where nothing "recurs," although a great deal "occurs." Listen to Stockhausen's *Gruppen* (1955-57) for a taste!

Following this swiftest of overviews, let us look at SOME OF THE PROBLEMS OF ELECTRONIC MUSIC:

1. The OUTRAGE of all Musicians Unions. The final "product" of most electronic music is A TAPE, and therefore Performers are eliminated!

Now, in some cases this is a good thing from the composers' point of view, given how difficult some performers can be, given the size of their egos and/or neuroses. The number of times the Maestro and I have wanted to eliminate both Miss Chlorina Wellersby and Mr. Claude Schlumpt for their "attitude beyond belief" when trying to rehearse new material!

However, when the Maestro and I have taken great efforts to try to deal with the above problem of performer elimination. it still hasn't worked.

We

1. Put the tape recorder on a lovely end table that had been tastefully strewn with rose petals and Lucetta's hand-painted shawl from her visit to Graceland.

2. Dressed up the McNallought boy in his good suit and put white gloves on him to come out and press the start button on the tape recorder.

But it

3. still failed.

The Four Square Gospel hall was empty by 8:17 p.m. as ther was NOTHING TO LOOK AT!

And the stink that old Herb Hogue raised (he's the president of the local Chezlee, Ont., Musicians Union, affiliated with the A.F. of M., the U.A.W., and the N.D.P.) about our campaign to deprive performers of work was very messy.

The truth of the matter is, however, that as BORING as it is to sit there in "the Hall" and watch people

I) blowing
ii) plucking
iii) scraping
iv) banging
v) what have you

it's better than sitting, staring at a tape recorder, all evening, even tho' it's sitting on a fine end table with a shawl of black velvet and the head of Elvis on it in paint that lights up in the dark.

PROBLEM NUMBER TWO

This problem applies not only to electronic music composers but to a lot of composers of modern music and that is this: THEY WRITE A LOT ABOUT WHAT THEY'RE TRYING TO DO!

There are a lot of very smart composers out there who write very intellectually complex music, but in order to REALLY UNDERSTAND IT, it is necessary to wade through a ton of verbiage about it that frequently requires a Philadelphia lawyer or an M.I.T. graduate engineer's degree.

My point is this, that if you have to do a lot of INTELLECTUAL RESEARCH before you

a) sit down in seat 37 at the F.S.G.H.

or

b) put on a CD or tape in the comfort of your favourite couch or sofa and LISTEN, it AIN'T WORTH IT.

Don't get me wrong! I never mind listening to music twice or thrice even in order to develop an appreciation of it.

BUT!

If I need a mathematical degree to appreciate a score on paper that equals the binomial theorem but still sounds like "whimsical fluff" OR if I need a doctorate in philosophy to comprehend all the words a composer wrote ABOUT the music he wrote, IS IT WORTH IT?

At some level, the MUSIC has to STAND (or fall, as the case my be) ON ITS OWN AND, simply and purely, be LISTENED TO.

I hear you, dear absorber of my thoughts, saying "There he goes again on his high horse, spouting off ..."

Well, that's true and I have avowed to stick to my overall aim, which is to get you OUT of your musical rut, and get you LISTENING to what is now quite OLD music of the 20th century, but

1. I can't help expressing my opinions.
2. That's precisely what I want to encourage you to do, dear reader, is LISTEN and EXPRESS YOURSELF!

Music (and the Arts in general) can only GET BETTER as we LISTEN and EXPRESS OURSELVES and that's all I'll say about that!

CHAPTER 12:
THE N.D.P. DEFEND WEIRDOS

First of all, let me assure you that there are no political biases in this book, one way or the other. I got into such trouble recently when, in an article on "Best Time to Fertilize," I praised the N.D.P. position *vis-à-vis* June.

By the N.D.P. of course I'm referring to that stirling and adventurous group of horticulturalists known as the NASTURIUM, DAHLIA & PANSY group.

Valiant upholders of neglected flowers, they were originally a breakaway branch from the CHEZLEE ROSE CONSORTIUM. They felt that roses got enough attention and between Valentine's Day, Mother's Day and "Apologies After Tiffs," their sales were high enough and that, as a flower, they didn't need a support group.

However, there were many less-well-known flowers with considerably lower sales records that did need encouragement and succour. They picked the Nasturtium, Dahlia and Pansy as representatives — archetypes, if you will — of less popular flora, even and especially extending to the underdogs of flowers (such as Dog Daisies and Queen Anne's Lace, considered a weed by some) and defended them, promoted them and took up their cause.

Gradually, over the years, the N.D.P. began to expand their horizons and became known as the promoters and defenders of all sorts of otherwise unknown, neglected, belittled, odd, weird and defenceless types and so, when it came to the Arts, and specifically Music, the N.D.P. Music Support Group (NDPMSG) went straight to the most way-out, experimental composers,who were willing to forge new horizons, go where human ears had not been taken before to lend them a boost! Needless to say, the N.D.P. have always been staunch and stalwart defenders of the works of the Maestro and myself and more often than not have been the sole members of the audience at some of our more daring premières.

Once again, at this juncture, I find myself compelled to remind the reader of what was said earlier — namely, that Modern is as old as the hills and there is a long history of weirdos going way back in this century.

During those amazing first 14 years of the 20th century (1900-1914), one helluva lot of things happened:

1. Picasso lost his perspective
2. Schoenberg BROKE with the past and became SERIAL or 12-TONE
3. There were all sorts of technical advances and improvements (especially toilets)
4. Stravinsky caused a RIOT

to mention a few.

And in 1913, a group of Italian artists known as FUTURISTS issued a MANIFESTO written up by their chief spokesperson, Luigi Russolo. The overall title of Russolo's Manifesto was THE ART OF NOISE, and I quote extensively:

"We must break out of this narrow circle of pure musical sounds and conquer the infinite variety of noise — sounds. We futurists have all deeply loved the music of the great composers, Beethoven and Wagner for many years wrung our hearts. But now we are satiated with them and derive much greater pleasure from ideally combining the noises of streetcars, internal combustion engines, automobiles and busy crowds, than from RE-HEARING for example, the *Eroica* or the *Pastoral.*

Do you believe it? In 1913 already!

This daring call to break with the past and look for sounds "which no ears had heard before" was answered by many and the N.D.P. have become their champions. Let us look at a mere few.

The first one we'll discuss became the kind of mascot of the N.D.P. and that is the American composer John Cage (1912-1992), who is said to belong to the ULTRAMODERN WING of this century. What makes my blood boil is that each of his three works that I will discuss here were all precedented right here in Chezlee, Ont., by the Maestro or myself and who has ever heard of the names Albani or Darling being associated with the Ultramodern wing of modern composers and given the respect and fame that John Cage has been given and deserves? (However, I let that rest!) Here's a quote:

"Cage attracted wide attention with his music for 'PREPARED PIANO'"

Cage's great invention was to muffle and alter the sound of the piano by inserting a variety of objects between the strings — to whit, rubber, felt, wood, screws, nuts, bolts etc. — and playing his pieces on it!

Well, this is a direct steal from the piano here at Obscuria. Colli had inherited it from his great-aunt Cora along with the family tendency NOT to be fastidious housekeepers. It was an old Flufenheimer manufactured down in Hinkelberg, Ont., and had been a fine instrument but what with Aunt Cora's loss of memory in her senior years and Colli's somewhat loose domestic policy there were more odd things inside that piano than there were keys (91 to be exact). From girdle stays to ancient flypaper rolls, there was enough junk inside that old Flufen to start a not-modest flea-market franchise. When Colli would sit down of a winter's evening at the crackled keyboard and render the second movement of Beethoven's sonata *Pathetique* or Schumann's *Traumerei* (which actually means "dreams"), they were indistinguishable from each other and unrecognizable in the extreme. Talk about a prepared piano. We've had one for years. Anyway, I don't mind that Cage gets all the credit so I'll leave it at that. I don't wish to sound bitter or resentful and the purpose of this book is to encourage you to listen to all types of Modern Music and Cage is one of the cornerstones of it so I won't say any more.

Another provocative work of Cage is his world-reknowned, revolutionary piece entitled *4'33"* (1952).

It is in three movements, titled I, II, and III and beside each Roman numeral is the length of time each movement should take, totalling four minutes and thirty three seconds. Also, beside each Roman numeral is the word *TACET*, which indicates NOTHING is to be played — or SILENCE.

ANY performer or performers can come out on to the concert stage with any instrument or instruments and the performer(s) and the audience(s) sit and listen to

a) the sound of their own breathing.

b) the air-conditioning system of the building (if it has one!).

c) internal, and/or external gas.

d) a distant fire engine if something as interesting as a devastating fire happens to occur in the *4'33"*.

e) ....

I'm sorry but I just can't continue with this list 'cause I'm that boiling mad!

In 1950, TWO YEARS BEFORE THE CAGE WORK, Colli and I organized a small student recital at the Methodist Church Sunday School Auditorium (because the Four Square Gospel Hall had been flooded due to a septic tank explosion).

In the second half of this nail-biting ordeal the young Miss Clevinia Slutledge got up to render a piece of Colli's entitled *Swamp and Bog Defections*, scored for piano, cracked mirrors (2) and a barrel of rainwater. Clevinia had always been subject to "nerves" and the moment she sat down at the keyboard she froze and remained immobile for 5 minutes and 17 seconds, during which there was the sound of

a) a lot of feet shuffling

b) old man Slutledge's under-the-breath swearing

c) external gaseous eruptions from the Maestro's quarters (he'd had Lucetta's Lima Delight for supper)

d) Slovenia Slutledge (Clevinia's mother) sniffling and sobbing (Clevinia had inherited her nerves)

e) what have you

But was this EARLIER and LONGER event in RADICAL INDETERMINACY bruited abroad on Reuters *et al?* Were the Maestro or myself lauded for our ultramodern advances in musicological quarterlies? Was there international acclaim? No. Not a bit!

The only record of this event was a small article on page 3, the inside page, of the *Chezlee Sez* that was entitled: DISASTROUS SILENCE AT LOCAL FIASCO

Sorry reader! I apologize! But it does upset me *du temps en temps*.

Trying to get back to the point, I would like to discuss another Cage composition, written for "A Butterfly in a Jar to be performed in an auditorium with open windows on a warm summer's evening and starts when the butterfly is released and lasts until (or if) the butterfly flys out one of the open windows."

That's it! That's the score! You're reading music, dear reader!

All I can say is ... PLEASE!

Have the proponents of modern experimental music never been to a concert at the Four Square Gospel Hall between June 1 and Sept. 30? Between bats, crickets, bullfrogs, a skunk, two weasels, a mouse nicknamed Monteverdi, a host of flies, bees and ladybugs, the Hall has functioned as a virtual zoo and yet ... and yet ...

You've had enough of my bile, dear reader, so I won't beg your indulgence further and I'll put Cage in his cage and move on. Don't get me wrong — we admire the man greatly, he's one of our heros, but a little credit where it's due would be nice.

There are tons of composers that Cage influenced with his new way of thinking about sound and music and performance and you'll find a list of them in the appropriate chapter. However, if you're just beginning to dabble in Modern Music and you're wanting to stick your big toe into the chilly waters of the WAY OUT, try Cage. He was really a "hippie" all his life and so was happiest in the '60s and early '70s when hippies were popular. I myself met him on the occasion of his 70th birthday and he was still wearing desert boots and denim. Now, if that doesn't tell you something ...

So in conclusion, rattle your musical cage with a bit of Cage and you may look at traditional music up to 1900, the music of our century, and, nay, all sound from A TOTALLY NEW AURAL PERSPECTIVE.

AN ESSAY
If MUSIC reflects the TIMES ... WHAT TIMES!!!

I'll never forget the tent caterpillar plague of '56. Them little suckers moved into Chezlee, Ont., (and environs, I might add), set up their tents (cobwebby monstrosities everywhere that made the whole county look like the set for Miss Haversham's dining room in *Great Expectations*) and proceeded to munch, crunch and gobble every single edible leaf, blade, veg or berry for miles. It was a devasting period in all of our lives and my compositional output during this gloomy time reflects the fear and turmoil, the angst and agony of those turged days.

Here are the titles of some of my works from that period:

Op 41, No. 3 — *Hommage à un dying pansy* (for contralto and bass clarinet)

Op 43, No. 17 — *Annus caterpillerus horribilus* (a choral and orchestral work, including 2 tractor motors and nails on blackboard)

Op 46, © — *When will it end?* (An SATB hymn, sung once at the Walmer Falls Gospel Hall, but the pastor took it personally re: his incumbency so it was never sung again)

Op 47, (I), (ii) and (iii) — An interactive piece for butter churn and any nasty pest, in three parts.

Parts (I) - Find the buggers

(ii) - Kill the buggers

And a choral ode, *CREMATORIUM/BUGGEROURIUM*

The above is a light sampling of my personal output during '56 and shows how the times influence art (or, in my case, music!).

So, dear reader, let us cast a swift birdseye view over this last 100 years known as the 20th century to see how its noises affected the sound of the music that was written. I have chosen to do a semi-artistic visual presentation, hitherto untried by any writer in my ken, to allow you to see (and FEEL) the FULL IMPACT of the times, letting your mind (and heart) meander around the century, till you feel its gist. And now here 'tis:

HONESTLY NOW, I ASK YOU,
What kind of music would you expect to come from an age like this???
I'm not saying it's been all bad. A few walls have come down
e.g. 1) the Berlin Wall 2) the Iron Curtain
3) Apartheid 4) Ciaocescu
5) the stone wall between the McCrumm's and the O'Raggity's

down past the abettoir, ending a century-old feud over property lines and a painting of Maggie O'Raggity's cow done by Merton McCrumm.

But, in general, it's been a pretty rough, turbulent time. Is it any wonder that the music of the modern age has created the impulse to insert earplugs?

However, in the midst of this modern cacophony have been some real gems, nuggets of musical gold well worth panning for.

Secondly (although, upon reflection I'm not sure we had a firstly) some composers have chosen to write counter to the age in which we live and have written some of the most peaceful, harmonious, sweet, nay even bland music ever heard. For example:

1) MUZACK

2) Yanni (pronounced Yawn-ee!)

3) Most New Age Music (it helps if you've had one too many Stoney Ripples)

4) Minimalist Music (based on 3 or 4 notes so it either lulls you to sleep or sends you flying over the cuckoo's nest)

5) My own *Nocturne for Harp and Kazoo based on Mating Calls of Male Bullfrogs* (although female bullfrogs find this composition fairly stimulating and have been known to procreate during a performance)

6) Music (in general) that has been written with the motivational force of...

a) We'll gather lilacs in the spring again (Ivor Novello)

or b) Ripples on the Quarry Pond - for 17 flutes, 5 pebbles and a wide tub of rainwater (needless to say, by yours truly)*

HOWEVER, there's one more point that is pushing my 39-cent Bic Ballpoint and that is this.

The "MUSIC THAT WE PREFER — 1600-1900" was the music of, by and for, the upper, upper class.

There were just as many wars (maybe more), plagues and natural devastations in those times, although maybe not quite as much noise till the Industrial Revolution got under way. But the music that any man, woman or child can listen to today in

a) concert halls

b) certain radio stations (CFMX or CBC 2 — that's its name this week)

c) very occasionally on TV hidden in the midst of all the "ME" TV crap

where any Tom, Dog or Harriet has their own (useless) show about nothing. d) your own CD player

*as yet, unperformed as I'm still looking for flautists no 12 and 15.

that music — I say, music from 1600-1900 — was

ONLY AVAILABLE LIVE FOR

1. Kings (and or Queens)
2. Popes (and their nephews)
3. Princes, Princesses, Earls, Barons, Marchesas (both kinds) and Etceteras (either)
4. In general, the RICH and ROYAL while the rest of the population — the peasants, the workers, the soldiers, the farmers and the milkmaids — had to be content with

a) a bit of a song at the pub with the accompaniment of a lute or mandolin (if they were lucky) or

b) a bit of a dance behind the barn to the tune of a vile (fiddle) and or drum (small) or

c) a marching song for the soldiers, as they trundled off to fight another war for 1, 2, 3 and 4 (see above)

It wasn't til the 19th century and THE RISE OF THE MIDDLE CLASS that they started having PUBLIC CONCERTS where, if they forked over their 7 Pfenig or 6 Sistersas, they could listen to the MUSIC once heard ONLY by RULERS who thought they were GOD and ROYALS trying to climb up the ladder.

The "DEMOCRACY" of the 20th century altered the course of MUSIC substantially, and that's why we're in a bit of a muddle *vis-à-vis* MODERN MUSIC and keep reaching for the Johnson and Johnson Rubber Ear Plugs! (Rubbermaid's are too hard and they hurt).

So, in conclusion, though not in short, it is the nature of the 20th century and its socio-economic and political ramifications that have affected the MUSIC of the MODERN age more so than our music has affected it (the age). So remember:

1. It's been a pretty rough century in many ways.
2. Be a little kinder to the music it has produced.
3. How would you feel if you'd been through two World Wars, a Depression, a Cold War and too many Andrew Lloyd Webber musicals?
4. Always try to understand the context in which a composer has written a piece of music and ask questions like:

i) Were there bombs or land mines going off in the back yard?

ii) Was he/she having trouble with a quarrelsome spouse/partner?

iii) Was he/she an elitist slob or pinko friend of the people?

iv) etc., etc.

In other words, GIVE MODERN MUSIC A CHANCE, FOR GOD'S SAKE!!

CHAPTER 13: CONTROL AND (WORSE) THE LACK OF IT

DRAWING CENSORED AS IT INVOLVES THE USE OF.....DEPENDS!!!

As I approach the period following WWII, it is with ginger steps and a great deal of trepitude, as it is a complex time. After any war, it's always messy and music is no exception, particularly when it's the second war and the world simply moved from a hot war to a cold one. However, that Roman descendant, that Zeus of musicologists, the dear Maestro himself, Colli Albani, has encouraged me to forge ahead and specifically has said "Give 'em a picture, Anthon — remember Confucius!" And so I introduce this chapter pictorially with a visual glimpse of two domiciles of a contrasting nature.

Here is OBSCURIA, our own humble abode:

OBSCURIA

Note the random, Joycean, free flow of the place.

Here is the apartment of G.D. Phineas:

G.D. PHINEAS' PLACE

Note the disciplined, ordered, right-angled, organized and somewhat anal ambience.

And there you have it, folks! The TWO CONTRASTING SCHOOLS of music following WWII.

1. INDETERMINACY — like Obscuria and
2. INTEGRATED SERIALISM — like G.D. Phineas's place.*

Let's discuss Number 2 first:

No. 2. CONTROL or INTEGRATED SERIALISM

Now, the details of exactly what "Integrated Serialism" is, I will not get into, dear average music lover, because it would

a) confuse you to tears

b) bore you to drink

c) make you throw up your hands and head off for Casino-rama.

What I will explain, however, is the principle:

BEFORE:

1. Composers would write down a piece of music on score paper, using the universally accepted language of music (called notation), which was FAIRLY specific and told you ALMOST everything you needed to know, but there was still A LOT OF ROOM left for INDIVIDUAL INTERPRETATION.

2. Composers would try to find a publisher to publish the composition. 3. They would look for a PERFORMER to

I) play the piece in a concert or ii) record the piece on a CD

*Just because we live in an indeterminate atmosphere does not mean we don't listen to the music of Number 2 — indeed, No. 2 music is among ourfaves, so we're not biased.

4. The composer would then BITE HIS (OR HER) NAILS, HOPE AGAINST HOPE THAT THE PERFORMER WOULD DO IT RIGHT*

In short, the COMPOSER had been in a very VULNERABLE POSITION, and SUBJECT TO THE WHIMS OF

I) the performer(s) (they have tons of whims)

ii) the publisher and of course,

iii) the audience (the whimsiest of the lot).

So, COMPOSERS WANTED MORE CONTROL. Here's how their thinking went:

A. In the 19th century, the Romantic movement went nuts, with individual interpretation gone amuck.

B. Schoenberg invented a nice, organized, mathematical system called SERIALISM or the 12-TONE SYSTEM.

C. His pupil Webern made it even more tight and controlled.

D. Let's go all out and CONTROL ABSOLUTELY EVERYTHING.

There were two ways to do this.

1. Eliminate the Performer — using electronic sounds, make a tape and just play it at a concert. It will always be THE SAME.

2. Tell, show, write EXACTLY EVERYTHING for the performer(s) to do so there's ABSOLUTELY NO ROOM FOR QUESTIONS OR PERSONAL INTERPRETATION and, in that way, every performance will be EXACTLY THE SAME.

The composers who chose to write music in this way would have loved to live in the G.D. Phineas place, where everything was highly organized and always in the same place.

Let's now look at the other way of composing music, which was

Number 1. INDETERMINACY — like Obscuria (our place).

The best way to tell you about this is to describe Stockhausen's *Piano Piece XI* (1956).

1. The score is published in three forms:

   a). In a roll packed in a cardboard carton.

   ii. With a wooden stand to put on a piano.

   3. On a board.

*How often have Colli and I sat in the back row of the Four Square Gospel Hall and got slivers in our cheeks from shifting and soaked three towels whilst a wannabe performer rendered one of our compositions. Several times I've had to stuff the *Chezlee Sez* in the Maestro's mouth so he wouldn't yell out "That's not the way it goes, you great NIG NOG WART-BRAINED S _ _ _ _!"

2. The score is 37" x 21"
3. There are 19 fragments or bits of pieces.
4. The performer plays them in WHATEVER ORDER he or she wants.
5. There are 6 different tempos
   6 different dynamic levels
   6 different types of touch (legato, staccato, etc.) and performers select what they like.
6. When one fragment has been played three times, the piece is over and, hopefully, the audience (if there is one) applauds.

So, with INDETERMINACY, so much is left "up to chance" that it has also come to be known as CHANCE MUSIC or ALEATORIC MUSIC.*

To really understand the music that many modern composers have written, it is necessary to READ WHAT THEY WROTE ABOUT THEIR MUSIC and in most cases you need a dictionary, a textbook on quantum theory, a physicist, an electrical engineer and a smart lawyer to get "the gist," as it were.

To show you what I mean, I'm going to give you a few quotes. You may

a) read them.
b) read them again.
c) ignore them and move on to the next chapter.
d) go for a jug of Stoney Ripple at the Ox & Udder or whatever your favourite local is.
e) phone a friend and discuss
   i) the weather
   ii) American politics and sex
   iii) sex apart from American politics
   iv) aphids and runner beans
f) listen to a nice tidy Mozart piano sonata with a moderate amount of personal interpretation.
g) write a letter to the *Chezlee Sez* complaining about the so-called Music Critic — Irvin Tornquist.

Anyway, here are three quotes under my headings:

Quote No. 1 — REASONABLY UNDERSTANDABLE

Pierre Boulez (Paris, 1975)

"I have often compared a work with the street map of a town; you don't change the map, you perceive the town as it is, but there are different ways of

*This is a wonderful comment to drop at intermission when you feel a performer has taken too many "chances" and failed (even with Bach) — you simply lower your eyelids to half mast and say "Too aleatoric."

visiting it. I find this comparison extremely suggestive, the work is like a town or labyrinth. A town is often a labyrinth too: when you visit it you choose your own direction and your own route; but it is obvious that you get to know the town, you need an accurate map and knowledge of the traffic regulations.

Personally, I have never been in favour of chance. I do not think that chance has much to contribute on its own account. So my idea is not to change the work at every turn nor to make it look like a complete novelty, but rather to change the viewpoints and perspectives from which it is seen while leaving its basic meaning unaltered."

Quote No. 2 — HAVEN'T GOT A CLUE

Yannis Xenakis (1955)

"Linear polyphony by its present complexity destroys itself. What one hears in reality is no more than a heap of notes in various registers.The enormous complexity prevents the hearer from following the criss-crossing of lines and has a macroscopic effect — an irrational and fortuitous dispersal of notes across the whole range of the sound spectrum. There is consequently a contradiction between the linear polyphonic system and the heard result which is surface mass. This inherent contradiction will disappear as soon as the independence of notes becomes clear. With the linear combinations and their polyphonic superpositions no longer operating, that which counts will be the statistic moment of the isolated states of transformation of components in a given moment. The macroscopic effect could be then controlled by the average of movements of the objects chosen by us. There results from it the introduction of the notation of the probability, implied elsewhere in this actual case of the combinatory calculus."

He went on to develop his ideas in a textbook called *Formalized Music* (1963) and when I'm able to understand the above paragraph I'll buy the book. (I've been working on it since 1971, so ...)

Quote No. 3 — JUST 'CAUSE I LOVE THIS ONE

Pierre Boulez in 1976, about to conduct Wagner's *Ring* at Bayreuth (the temple Wagner built for the production of his operas), said:

"I once said the most elegant solution of the problem of opera was to blow up the opera houses and I still think this is true. Opera is the area before all others in which things have stood still. As I see it, *Wozzeck* is the last opera ..." ("What an end!" says the Maestro, who's just asked me to join him at the Ox & Udder for a pint. So I think I will.)

So what is my point, dear valiant reader (if you opted to wade through these quotations)?

IF YOU HAVE TO
a) READ A BOOK
b) UNDERSTAND QUANTUM THEORY
c) HAVE AN I.Q. HIGHER THAN STEVEN HAWKING
IN ORDER TO APPRECIATE A PIECE OF MUSIC, why not
a) take a course in glass-leading.
b) have intercourse with a close friend (there are seven meanings in the dictionary, so take your pick).
c) enjoy a light lunch of fresh leaf lettuce, lox and Loganberry wine
d) listen to Rimsky-Korsakov's *Scheherezade* and fantasize about ...
e) turn the page for the next chapter.

Note: The list of composers and compositions, both CONTROLLED and NOT, will be found in the appropriate chapter (whatever that is — I can't look it up now, 'cause I have to go!).

CHAPTER 14:
QUOTES AND THE K.I.S.S. PRINCIPLE

There's only so much CONTROL — or worse, LACK OF CONTROL — that a person, or society or music can take. (I remember a period of time after the annual Barbequed Baked Beans Competition in which I was the sole judge that I personally do not wish to relive ever again, thank you very much).

By the 1960s composers in general said "Enough of serialism, already"

or "I'm tired of the 12-Tone method"

or "Remember when music was ENJOYABLE and didn't require a PhD. to listen to it?"

or "etcetera."

And so, two (2) new trends started developing and they were:

1. Quotation Music

and 2. Minimalism (or following the K.I.S.S. principle; i.e. "Keep It Simple, Stupid!")

This time, I shall discuss number one firstly and then secondly, number two.

1. QUOTATION MUSIC

Essentially, in a nutshell, this is music where composers use earlier music as the material for a new composition, but change it somehow.

Well, there was a general WHOOP DEE DOO among composers when they realized that they could use anything from Gregorian chant to Bach to Brahms to Stravinsky to whatever as the "material" for their music and fool around with it. Just as in the '60s the hippies were fooling around with magic mushrooms and each other and generally casting off all the "old rules," so composers took off the "GIRDLE" of SERIALISM and let their music all hang out, as it were, and took a thousand years of great music and fooled around with it. Well, all Hell (or Heaven) broke loose and they had a ball!

However, there is an important note to make here and that is this:

When composers "QUOTED" earlier music, THEY SAID SO and SAID WHOSE MUSIC THEY WERE USING! In other words, they were:

a) honest
b) not guilty of plagiarism
c) not robbing anybody of royalties.

HOWEVER, as I've mentioned before, THERE WAS, AND IS, ONE NOTABLE EXCEPTION who "quotes" melodies by other composers without giving them either

a) the credit
or b) the royalties

AND WORSE, he claims the tunes as his own as if he were the cleverest fellow since since old Elmer Eebles figured out a way to milk three cows at once using only two milking machines. (And that you've got to SEE to believe.)

But we don't much like the thought of a bunch of LAWYERS tromping all over our petunia patch and frightening the horses and accusing us of LIBEL or SLANDER, so I won't mention his name(s) and I'd best not say any more except

SHAME ON YOU, _ !!!

Fortunately, the man keeps saying he's stopping writing music and the world can only heave a heartfelt sigh of relief. Would to God some of his gazillions of dollars could be used to foster the development of truly "original" compositions or, if he were an honest man, he would 'fess up and give some bucks to the descendants of composers who should be gettin' somethin' from their granddaddy's genius and estate.

Anyway, enough of that! I didn't want to get fired up in vicious bile or negativity. This is a positive book, encouraging the reader to listen to Modern Music and if you want to pay the $95.00 plus P.S.T. plus G.S.T. to sit for a couple of hours and hear hundred-year-old composers' works badly quoted, that's up to you. As I said before, I'll say no more.

NOW, let's look at the Second Trend of the '60s, namely: MINIMALISM (or following the K.I.S.S. principle).

These composers the Maestro and I have not only admired but have been greatly influenced by in our own not-insignificant output. The Keep It Simple, Stupid! phrase has been an oft-shouted motto around here in Obscuria, to say nothing of a slight variation of it that both of us have heard shouted AT us on more than one occasion: namely "Kiss Off! Stupid Simpletons!" We smile and nod in the certain knowledge that they are actually congratulating us for our K.I.S.S. *modus operandi*, but simply, in their ignorance calling it K.O.S.S. and not K.I.S.S.

The MINIMALISTS (namely La Monte Young, Terry Riley, Steve Reich and Philip Glass) had beefs!

The BEEFS of the MINIMALISTS:

1. Modern Music is getting TOO COMPLEX.
2. Modern Music Composers are
   a) highly educated
   b) extremely intellectually oriented
3. Modern Music is performed by a group of ELITE Musicians who are the ONLY ONES who could possibly figure out the COMPLEX INTRICACIES of new music.
4. Modern Music is listened to by a SMALL CLIQUE (mostly fellow composers).

THEREFORE, THE MINIMALISTS SAID:

A) MUSIC SHOULD BE SIMPLER
B) MUSIC SHOULD BE UNDERSTOOD
C) MUSIC SHOULD BE UNDERSTOOD BY UNTRAINED LISTENERS

Some of them, like Philip Glass, even dabbled in Pop and Rock-like sounds. Lucetta particularly loves the music of this period as she used to be the lead singer and rhythm guitarist in an all-girl rock and roll band called Lucetta's Lollapaloozas. Unfortunately, their professional life was brief, as Lulu got pregnant and Lucille got a job, so they broke up.

The Maestro's and my own experiments in MINIMALISM have had a variety of reactions, ranging from "Thank God" to "Thank God it's Over!"

In '73 we premiered a multi-media work called MIDDLE SEA for

a) one note on the piano, namely middle C
b) a still-life painting of one apple
c) the smell of popcorn
d) Herb Crunchley on drums.

We didn't quite get to the actual end of the piece, as the easel supporting the painting collapsed and Una Byfould starting beating Herb on the head with her umbrella (although I must give Una credit, as she did her somewhat sadistic beating in perfect rhythm). Rumours were rampant as to an earlier possible liaison between the two that had soured but Una claims it was the 337th time that the McNallought boy hit Middle C in succession that put her "over the edge," as she was quoted saying in the Sydenburgh County Jail cell, where she served half an hour for public mischief.

However, the MINIMALISTS did eliminate complexity and adopted a SIMPLER APPROACH.

Now, while the Maestro and I do laud their efforts, never being ones to be overly intellectual or to complicate matters by verbal or musical overdosing, there are, however, having said that, a few problems.

PROBLEMS of MINIMALISM:

1. Audiences can tire of hearing only 4 notes over and over again, no matter how many variations of these 4 occur.

2. People who ONLY KNOW 4 NOTES can become international stars! For example, YANNI (should be spelled "YAWN-EE,") who gets a symphony orchestra the size of Texas to play the C-major scale up and down for half an hour and because, "he's cute," people pay their money and enjoy it. Why, even our Lucetta sits and listens to this crap and sighs longingly, hoping for some kind of extra-musical liaison with the composer-slash-performer (altho' richer women than Lucetta have already claimed him and lost).

3. One tends to find that halfway through listening to MINIMALIST MUSIC, you're out behind the barn shredding asparagus stalks and you don't remember HOW you got there! Was it

a) subliminal suggestions?
or b) musical hypnosis with suggestions?
or c) you get bored?

But if you're just venturing into the serious music of the 20th century, MINIMALISM isn't a bad place to start.

You can SURE understand it at FIRST listening and you SOON find out if you like it or not. So give it a try!

CHAPTER 15:

PLURALISM IS NOT POLYGAMY

The reason I've used such a controversial title for this chapter that essentially deals with music from circa 1970 to the present (now) (as in today), is because of the incredible furor the Maestro created when asked to address the Presbyterian Women's Crochet, Catechism and Cultural Pursuits Club (always abbreviated to the P.W.C.C.C.P.C.).

They always regarded it as a real "coup" to get the Maestro as speaker because he could hit them at all three levels of their tri-purpose organization. His knowledge of tatting and the best crochet hooks is locally renowned; he is fluent in Knoxian theological positions, having been reared in the heart of Italy's wine region by Scottish Calvinists; and his ability to speak on any subject relating to music is internationally respected and sought after.

That fateful fall when he last spoke to the P.W.C.C.C.P.C., he had chosen a deliciously tri-partite menu of mental delights for "the girls." It was

A. Tough Tatting Knots and how to get out of them.

B. Knox KNOCKS KNOWLEDGE: Presbyterianism and anti-intellectualism.

C. PLURALISM: Where it's *at* in the Arts today.

The Right Reverend T.C. Tippley was the incumbent of St. Cudfort's at that time and happened to be in the rectory office at the time of the Maestro's lecture.

In retrospect, Colli always thought that "Old T.C.T." (as he was known from behind) had had his ear cocked at the door during Part 2 of his presentation, wanting to make sure there were no heretical statements made or any untoward slights at Calvin or Knox or Presbyterianism in general. However, it was when the Maestro commenced the third part of his three-hour lecture with the statement:

"Ladies! Pluralism is where it's at in the Arts today, as ..."

That's as far as he got. "Old T.C.T." shot out of the church office like a lion starved for lunch. He berated the astounded lecturer, who, shocked by this sudden and totally unwarranted attack, was reduced to stunned stuttering. After hitting the Maestro over the head several times with the organist's copy of *Hymns of Praise and Worship* (the thick one), "Old T.C.T." chased the Maestro down the left aisle through the vestibule and heaved him out and down the front steps. It took Peter Blurgells, the vet, two stitches to mend the Albani elbow which, despite the pain, was bent repeatedly après the incident at the Ox & Udder as the wounded professor sought solace with gallons of Stoney Ripple Ale.

"Pluralism is not Polygamy" the Maestro was heard yelling long into the night, long after last call, and it is as a kind of tribute to Colli's unfortunate suffering for the sake of art that I have titularly named the present chapter.

"If it's not polygamy, then what exactly is Pluralism?" I can hear echoing through the collective recesses of your minds. Well, that's what I'm about to tell you.

DEFINITIONS OF PLURALISM:

1. Everybody's doing their own thing and it's O.K.
2. Bit o' this, Bit o' that.
3. There's more than one way to skin a cat!
4. You can mix and match any old way of composing from anytime and anywhere.
5. There's *no* "Hit Chart" with "Who's #1 this week?" There are many charts, with *many* hits.
6. It does not mean that one is allowed or encouraged to have more than one spouse, either simultaneously (which is considered bigamy or trigamy or polygamy) or subsequently (which is called serial polygamy and is practised by many in our society and was approved of by the Romanian Orthodox Church during the reign of Queen Marie circa the turn of the century, when they allowed three subsequent marriages and divorces, so that you could be at a reception with your present spouse, see your "ex" at the bar with her next, and be on the hunt for number three!).

7. In Music it means there are Minimalists, Serial Determinists, Indeterminists, Quotationists, Neo Classicists, Post-Modernists, straight Serialists, gay Serialists, Post Romantics, Plagiarists (like _ _ _ _ _ _ _ _ _ _ _ _ _), Rock and Rollists, Experimentalists, New-Experimentalists, Untalented People Who Suck Up To Awards Committees To Get Grants To Write Crapists and guys who combine all of the above (and there are more!!!).

WHY DOES PLURALISM REIGN IN OUR AGE?

To this resounding query I succinctly respond:

1. We're TOO CLOSE to living, fresh music to sort out the wheat from the chaff, as it were, so we're open to all till TIME judges who actually were the greats of our time.

2. NEVER BEFORE IN HISTORY has there been so much music available to so many composers by which to be influenced.

3. NEVER BEFORE IN HISTORY have there been SO MANY COMPOSERS and it's hard to sort out the "Greats" from the "Not-so's," the "ingrates" and the "totally talentless," although I do have a few suggestions for the last category.

"WHO ARE THE PLURALISTS?" you ask.

They are:

a) old guys who are still living and are either

i) doing their same old thing

or

ii) trying out new things

b) middle-aged guys who are in the prime of their own thing

c) young upstarts and wannabees who are willing to try anything.

The one thing they have in common is that they are all LIVING, which makes it tough for the music historian to write objectively about them. Distance is required and only age and time can provide that! (Besides, we don't want any more libel suits! We've had enough of those!)

Now, for specific pluralists, I suggest you check the appropriate chapter, whatever it is, and check some of them out.

The other suggestion I have is to try composing some music yourself. Since it's an age of pluralism and anything and everything is O.K., why not give it a try, particularly if you have a bent in that direction?

Neither Colli nor I ever intended to be composers, but given the state of art today, initially said: "Why not?" and believe it or not we have outlived our allotted "15 minutes of fame" and even, in some parts, moved on to infamy. So give it a try. Here are some suggestions:

SUGGESTIONS FOR SELF-COMPOSITION:

1. A minimalist work for Jew's Harp (see how long a piece you can write before you are shot).
2. A "quotation" opus containing Bach, Boogie, Berg and Rhubarb (but remember: Give credit where due).
3. A cereal composition using Corn Flakes, Bran, Count Chocula, Cheerios and a bathroom plunger.
4. What have you ...!

See what I mean?

It's an age of pluralism.

Cole Porter wrote a lovely show about it called *Anything Goes* and it could be no truer of any age than of our very own.

Never before has music been so

Unfettered

Unshackled

Unruled

Unusual

Unbelievable

So loosen your musical girdle, let down your artistic hair and open up to MODERN MUSIC and ALL SOUND*

*I've just heard the sound of the Desoto warming up in the barn-slash-garage and we've got eight minutes to get to last call at the Ox & Udder, so I'm off ...

A COMMENT
(CERTAIN *ASSPECKS* (olde English sp) OF MODERN MUSIC

A. THE GRAND CANYON SPLIT

COMPOSERS versus THE PUBLIC

If you think Modern music is "Weird" now, in 1999, just imagine what people thought back then when it was first performed in the 1910s and on.

In the one "corner" or the "ring" of culture, you had

THE COMPOSER

a) wanting to write something NEW and ORIGINAL, but...

b) inheriting an old system of music that had pretty well dried up, so...

c) he (or she) starts looking for alternatives and, admittedly, in the course of that search comes up with some pretty wild and wacky possibilities, that seem pretty weird to!

THE GENERAL LISTENING PUBLIC, who

a) have been contentedly paying their 2 pounds, 3 shillings to listen to Bach, Beethoven, Brahms and Bizet, who then are ...

b) suddenly confronted with Schoenberg's 12-Tone composition or a Charles Ives piece written in two different keys simultaneously, and they say

c) "What the H_ _ _ is going on? I can't stand that crap.
I can't hum the tune.
It's not easy or simple! It's complex!
I haven't the vaguest idea what it's about"
so
a RIFT
a CHASM
a GRAND CANYON SPLIT
was created between the COMPOSER and the GENERAL PUBLIC!

I must interject at this juncture and say that Chezlee, Ont., remains one of the few exceptions to this general rule.Due largely to the tireless efforts of Eunida, Una, Beryle, Clarice, Harriett as well as the other "girls" of the Chezlee Parnsip and Arts Fest (C.P.A.F.), new and original compositions have always been included in practically every concert that has occurred at the Four Square Hall over the last number of years.Granted, the modern stuff has been relegated to the second half of the concert, leaving it as a post-intermission option, although we did find (myself and the five audience members that stayed for the premières in Part II) that if we opened the windows, those that left could still hear quite well at the Ox & Udder next door. (The down side was that we could also hear them and that could be somewhat disconcerting during a pianissimo passage.)

But I do thank the "girls" for their stellar work in helping to bridge the gap between the composer (myself) and the public (the rest of the inhabitants of Chezlee, Ont.) and for exposing them (the public) to lots of Modern Music. At a recent fête, the attendance doubled for the second half, and all 10 of them seemed to enjoy it, even though Hervey Bumsteed's remark about cows flying o'er my head was uncalled for.

Anyway, to return to the point, while Chezlee, Ont., is an exception, for the most part,

THE GENERAL PUBLIC STOPPED LISTENING. They refused to pay the $2.75 for the seats and were totally unwilling to give MODERN MUSIC a try, so THE RIFT GREW AND REMAINS TO THIS DAY!

So who's been listening to Modern Music since 1900, you may well ask? Who (apart from the aforementioned Chezlee, Ont. group) indeed?

The answer is twofold:

1. Composers of Modern Music started forming groups or societies of composers of modern music and succinctly and ingeniously calling

themselves THE COMPOSERS OF MODERN MUSIC SOCIETY(S) and played their music for each other. All four or 26 or however-many-of-them would sit around and listen to each other's stuff and say "Ooh, I like that. I think I'll try a bit of that in my next piece" and so became

a) ISOLATED
b) INSULAR
c) INDIFFERENT
and
d) Frankly didn't give a damn what the public thought.

2. The second group of people who listened to Modern Music were the Mothers, Fathers,
Sisters, Brothers,
Spouses (Either),
Close Friends, or...
One-Night Stands
of the composer — and a lot of them only came once!

This radical new music was the cause of much domestic, familial, and relational consternation, giving rise to remarks like

1. "I raised you to write this?"
2. "Am I not satisfying you somehow in our relationship that would cause you to write that?"
3. "As a brother, I love and respect you. But as a composer I ... (censored!)"
4. "I'm going to the motel now so I'll see you there after this (XXX) is finished and believe me I expect more than 50 bucks for havin' to put up with that (XXXX)."

As the century bombarded on, the GRAND CANYON SPLIT between the composer(s) and the general public widened further and further and both suffered from the lack of exposure to the other.

AND IT IS THE AVOWED PURPOSE OF THIS BOOK TO
BRIDGE THE GAP
FILL THE CHASM
EXPOSE EACH TO THE OTHER
SO THAT

1. The GENERAL PUBLIC will LISTEN to Modern Music and
2. The Composers of Modern Music will listen to the comments of the General Public and together NEW MUSIC MAY BE BORN, the general public's ears enriched, and the composers won't have to drive cab on the night shift.

B GRANT'S TOMB (HE WHO PAYS THE PIPER, PICKS...)

Here's the question:
How do composers of music

- pay the rent or mortgage?
- feed themselves (and the kids)?
- buy new clothes?
- save up for their retiremen?
- have the occasional ale at the local?

Up to 1900 (roughly), composers of music worked for
KINGS, QUEENS
POPES, PRINCES etc. etc.
the rich and royal, powerful potentates who said "Write me a symphony (in MY honour) and I'll give you room and board for six months."

As things started changing in the 19th century and Kings and Queens were teetering and tottering and the middle class was rising higher and higher, composers got their money from

a) the occasional commission from a Baronet or Viscontessa (with jewels to sell).
and b) the "gate" from public concerts.
and c) royalties from published works.

Now, this system was working reasonably well, particularly in the 19th century when composers (and artists in general) were considered to be the great PROPHETS OF THE AGE

Remember from my last book? If you don't, just turn the page for a little reminder chart.

WHO'S TOP DOG?

1-450 Roman Empire — Caesar (sometimes Augustus)
450-1000 Dark Ages — Nobody
1000-1600 Medieval & Renaissance — the Church (in general)
1600-1725 Baroque — Kings (and/or Queens)
1725-1825 Classical — Kings, Queens and Philosophers (the Age of Enlightenment)
1825-1900 Romantic — COMPOSERS, AUTHORS, PAINTERS & SCULPTORS

In the century preceding the one we're in now, ARTISTS were considered to be

a) the ones with that special connection to the world beyond.

b) the "great ones" of their age.

c) those who could command top dollar at the box office.

d) the ones who made both men and ladies swoon in ecstasy, faint in frenzy, follow in ferrow, and try to rip their underwear off.

Well, in our century, SCIENCE, TECHNOLOGY, POLITICS and WAR knocked the stuffing out of the importance of the artist and when the arts "RAN OUT" and "DRIED UP" and artists had to find NEW WAYS of making music and art in general, they quickly

FELL IN ESTEEM and were replaced by the heroes of the 20th century.

And WHO are the HEROES of the 20th century?

THE HEROES OF THE 20TH CENTURY (IN ORDER OF IMPORTANCE):

1. Presidents (unless they're having sexual problems), Prime Ministers, (and Dictators)
2. Scientists, Inventors, Medical Researchers
3. Bill Gates
4. Movie Stars, T.V. Stars, Rock & Roll Stars
5. Madonna
6. The Media
7. Sports Stars
8. Business Magnates and the OLD MONEY rich
9. The *Nouveau Riche*
10. Your humble artists like myself (starving composers and Betsy Brack, the lady down Concession 17 who does enamelled milk cans with flowers on and tries to sell them at the Fall Fair and Furrowing Competition — unsuccessfully, I might add)

SO WHO SUPPORTS THE MODERN COMPOSER?

How does he or she pay his bills such as U.I., Hydro, Gas etc.?

The answer, once again, amazingly, is twofold:

A. UNIVERSITIES!

Most modern composers have to teach in order to survive so they become a "professor of music" at a university and compose on the side. Universities also have a lot of realyl good performing students who are willing to play anything put in front of them (particularly if it will help their mark or grade average for the year) so students perform the compositions of a professor for other students and other professors, who are also composers and everybody's happy and the UNIVERSITY foots the bill!!

B. GRANTS

You may wonder why, at the beginning of this section I titled it GRANT'S TOMB — a droll reference to the resting place of an American political hero. You will soon see as I explain the *10+-* of GRANTS, in the following concise and logical order:

1. Democratic governments feel they must "support the arts."

2. They set up an ARTS COUNCIL made up of government appointees who spread into a plethora of sub-committees who hold numerous meetings to decide the format for the application forms that the artist may obtain (if they hear about them) and fill out (if they are able to because they are highly complicated), and apply for A GRANT.

The sub-committee then meets to make recommendations to the larger group of committee heads (or chairs as the case may be, denoting the opposite part of the anatomy) who then make recommendations to the COUNCIL (general) and eventually a form is sent (usually) to the artist indicating whether he or she

a) GOT THE GRANT

and b) IF YES, HOW MUCH?

(Grants, by the way, are never enough to live on so the composer still has to teach all those wretched students, but a GRANT does help with repairing weeping tiles in the basement or a new lawn mower with a grass-collector bag.)

You will note, in the objective presentation of how the grant system works above, I studiously avoided any kind of personal comment or indication as to how I felt about it, but, perhaps, dear reader, you would be kind enough to permit a slight puncture in the scientific method otherwise observed in the "slim"* volume and does colour with a touch of blush the black and white objectivity strictly adhered to. However, don't ya think it was a bit easier when the Pope said "Listen Leo, about the ceiling, I think you should..." than to receive a communique, like this?

Office of the Administrator
And Disbursement of Funding
For the Purposes of the Propagation
Of cultural pursuits by Composers.

Dear Sir or Madam,

Upon careful consideration of your application by a delegation of sub-pan- and general committees it is, to wit, heretofo and notwithstanding, the considered opinion of said committees aforementioned that your application for a grant in order to write a *Quintet for Five Reeds* based on actual recordings of loon cries on Lake Muskog has been DENIED. You will not receive a single sou from us. However, we are giving a trip to Honolulu for two to the lovely Miss Beatrice Bodace in order to allow her to pursue and develop a concept for her idea of the possibility of a work and/or piece on Mating Rituals in Pacific Islands, and, as chief chairperson, I will be accompanying Miss Bodace to Hawaii and assisting her in her research. Please feel free to apply again. I remain,

The Chair

*Your quote, Catherine.

CHAPTER 16:
THE LISTENER'S GUIDE, FROM O.K. TO WACKY TO WAY OUT

The O.K. Composers:

Samuel Barber	1910-1981	Take your pick
Béla Bartok	1881-1945	Take your pick
Alban Berg	1885-1935	*Wozzeck*
Lennox Berkeley	1903-1990	Take your pick
Leonard Bernstein	1918-1990	*West Side Story*
Benjamin Britten	1913-1976	*Death in Venice*
Chan Ka Nin	1949-	Take your pick
Aaron Copland	1900-1990	*Billy the Kid*
Claude Debussy	1862-1918	Take your pick
Edward Elgar	1857-1934	*Pomp and Circumstance*
Lukas Foss	1922-	*Time Cycle*
Alberto Ginastera	1916-1983	Take your pick
Henryk Górecki	1933-	*Symphony No. 3*
Paul Hindemith	1895-1963	*Mathis der Maler*
Scott Joplin	1868-1917	Pick any ragtime
Aram Khachatarian	1903-1978	*Spartacus*
Wilhelm Killmayer	1927-	*Hölderlin-Lieder*
Erich Korngold	1897-1957	*Die Töte Stadt*
Gary Kulesha	1954-	Take your pick
Alexina Louie	1949-	Take your pick
Nikolai Medtner	1880-1951	Piano works
Darius Milhaud	1892-1974	*Suite Scaramouche*
Federico Mompou	1893-1987	*Canción y danza*
Meredith Monk	1942-	Take your pick
Erik Nordgren	1913-1992	Sountrack of Bergman's *Wild Strawberries*
Ignace Paderewski (also a Polish prime minister)	1860-1941	Take your pick
Arvo Pärt	1935-	Take your pick
Francis Poulenc	1899-1963	*Dialogue des Carmelites*
Sergei Prokofiev	1891-1953	*Romeo and Juliet*
Sergei Rachmaninoff	1873-1943	*Piano Concerto No. 3*
Maurice Ravel	1875-1925	Take your pick
Terry Riley	1935-	Take your pick

Erik Satie	1866-1925	*Gymnopédies*
Arnold Schoenberg	1874-1951	*Pierre Lunaire*
Alexandre Scriabin	1872-1915	Take your pick
Dmitri Shostakovich	1906-1975	Symphonies
Jean Sibelius	1865-1957	*Finlandia*
Richard Strauss	1864-1949	*Salome*
Igor Stravinsky	1882-1971	See Chapter 8
Virgil Thomson	1896-1989	*Four Saints in Three Acts*
Heitor Villa-Lobos	1887-1959	*Bachianas Brasileiras*
Anton Webern	1883-1945	Take your pick
Ralph Vaughan Williams	1872-1958	Take your pick

The Wacky Composers:

John Adams	1947-	*Nixon in China*
Tomas Adés	1971-	*Powder Her Face*
George Crumb	1929-	*Music for a Summer Evening*
Luigi Dallapiccola	1904-	*Volo di Notte*
Henri Dutilleux	1916-	Take your pick
John Harbison	1938-	Take your pick
Arthur Honegger	1892-1955	*Pacific 231*
Charles Ives	1874-1954	*Concord Sonata*
Léos Janácek	1854-1928	Pick an opera
Oliver Knussen	1952-	Walt Whitman settings
Zoltán Kodály	1882-1967	*Soffelgio* materials
György Kurtag	1926-	*Sayings of Peter Bornemisza*
Witold Lutoslawski	1913-	Take your pick
Bruno Maderna	1920-	*Notturno*
Bohuslav Martinu	1890-1959	Take your pick
Gian Carlo Menotti	1911-	*Amahl and the Night Visitors*
Carl Nielsen	1865-1931	Symphonies
Karol Szymanowski	1882-1937	*King Roger*
Toru Takemistsu	1930-1996	Take your pick
Tan Dun	1957-	*Marco Polo*
Marc-Anthony Turnage	1960-	*Greek*
John Weinzberg	1913-	Take your pick
Judith Weir	1954-	Take your pick

The Way-Out Composers

George Antheil	1900-1959	*Ballet Méchanique*
Milton Babbitt	1906-	Take your pick
Luciano Berio	1925-	Take your pick
Harrison Birtwistle	1934-	*Punch and Judy*
John Cage	1912-1992	See Chapter 13
Cornelius Cardew	1936-1981	*Music for his "Scratch" Orchestra*
Elliott Carter	1908-	
Henry Cowell	1897-1965	Take your pick
Peter Maxwell Davies	1934-	*Eight Songs for a Mad King*
Hans Werner Henze	1926-	Take your pick
André Jolivet	1905-1974	Take your pick
György Ligeti	1923-	*Le grand Macabre*
Oliveir Messiaen	1908-1992	*Quartet for the End of Time*
Luigi Nono	1924-	*Intolleranza*
Krzystov Penderecki	1933-	Take your pick
Murray Schafer	1933-	Take your pick
Alfred Shnitke	1934-	Take your pick
Karlheinz Stockhausen	1928-	Take your pick
Michael Tippett	1905-	Take your pick
Edgard Varése	1883-1965	*Ionisation*
William Walton	1902-1983	*Façade*
Yannis Xenakis	1922-	Take your pick
John Taverner	1944-	Take your pick

The "Pop"ular Serious Composers

Irving Berlin	1888-1992	Songs
Gavin Bryars	1943-	*Jesus' Blood Has Never Failed Me Yet*
John Corigliano	1938-	Soundtrack for *The Red Violin*
George Gershwin	1898-1937	*Rhapsody in Blue*
Philip Glass	1937-	Take your pick
Fritz Kreisler	1875-1962	Violin virtuoso pieces
Henri Mancini	1924-	*The Pink Panther*

Paul McCartney	1942-	*Liverpool Oratorio*
Ennio Morricone	1931	Soundtrack for *The Mission*
Michael Nyman	1944-	Soundtrack for *The Piano*
Carl Orff	1895-1982	*Carmina Burana*
Astor Piazzolla	1921-1992	Pick any tango
Cole Porter	1891-1964	Songs
Giacomo Puccini	1858-1924	Operas
Steve Reich	1936-	Take your pick
Nino Rota	1911-1979	Soundtrack for *The Godfather*
Stephen Sondheim	1930-	*A Little Night Music*
John Philip Sousa	1932-	*The Stars and Stripes Forever*
Andrew Lloyd Webber	1948-	Take your pick (He did!)
Kurt Weill	1900-1950	Songs
John Williams	1932-	Soundtrack of any Steven Spielberg or George Lucas film

CHAPTER 17: TERMS AND IMPRESSION-MAKERS FOR INTERMISSON CHIT-CHAT

I think one of the major reasons why most people don't support concerts involving Modern Music is that they

DON'T KNOW WHAT TO SAY AT INTERMISSION.

The barren puerility of "loved it!" or "hated it!" doesn't quite cut it, if you're trying to

a) make an impression
2) secure a promotion at work
iii) get a date for coffee and what-have-you *aprés* the concert
IV) be heard saying brilliant and insightful things

Well, once again, the Maestro has come to our aid and contributed majorly to the two lists of this chapter. These pages are the ones you should photocopy and shove in your purse, handbag, fanny pack (usually worn as a crotch pouch) etc. so they are easily accessible in an emergency if you're suddenly called upon to express an opinion about a work by Xenakis, or Stockhausen's latest opus.

In awkward situations like this, simply stall with an "It's time for my pill — just a minute please." As you search for your medication (a breath mint would serve nicely as what you're looking for), cast your eye quickly down the LIST STUFFED IN YOUR PURSE so that having "popped your pill," you can say

"Xenakis' stochastic approach has always intrigued me! 'Scuse please, gotta run!" or "Since Stockhausen's *Kontakte* (1959-60) combining both electronic music and *musique concrète*, I feel strongly, and appreciate deeply, his expansion well beyond the horizons of total serialism. Don't you think ?"

Responses of this sort usually cause the questioner to suddenly remember a hitherto-forgotten dental appointment and never again query you about anything so that at intermission you can quietly drink your gin martini in peace and solitude while others around you whisper behind their programs, "I wonder what HE thought of the first half???"

First of all:

A USEFUL LIST OF TERMS *VIS-À-VIS* MODERN MUSIC:

integral serialism	everything's controlled
indeterminancy	who knows?
Serialism	a regular T.V. show ? a fondness for Koko Puffs ? No! Look up *The Fertilizer Hits the Fan* (Chapter 7)

aleatoric	it's up to you
atonal	remember what music used to sound like? — this doesn't
bitonal	it goes both ways
polytonal	this goes every which way
tonal	nice !
chromaticism	a pain in the joints with lots of #'s and *b*'s
neo-'whatever'	bring out your old party dress and tart it up with cuffs and collars
post-'whatever'	what comes after (or before Bran Flakes)
contemporary music	what's being written NOW!
serious music	this is no laughing matter
Dada	first words uttered by a baby
Gebrauchmusick	this literally means useful music! So what's the rest? Useless ?
dissonance	sounds dreadful
consonance	sounds nice
assonance	behaving stupidly
dodecaphonic, 12-Tone	see *Fertilizer* (Chapter 7) and Schoenberg
electronic music	music that's plugged in
quotation music	stealing!
Minimalism	how to make a mountain out of a molehill
ethnomusicology	anything other than WASP or Dead White Guys' Music
expressionism	using music as emotional Ex-Lax
impressionism	you need new glasses
intestinalism	a parasite of the lower colon
functionalism	if it's no use, it doesn't matter
futurism	pre-W.W. I, largely Italian revolutionaries gave a *Concert of Noises* on June 15, 1914 in London (weird)
improvisation	make it up
intonation	if you don't have it, you're tone deaf
incantation	a spell sung by a Wicca or Warlock
microtonal	teeny-tiny tones, who can tell the difference?
mixed-media	read magazines, listen to the radio and watch TV at the same time
modernism	as old as the hills
musique concrète	what a cement mixer sounds like
New Music	the composer is usually alive and sitting in

	the audience (sometimes in drag to disguise his presence so he'll miss the tomatoes, altho' usually it's a loose-fitting wig and velcroed dress just in case there's kudos)
noises	rude
patronage	gone, by and large, but if interested please send cheques to yours truly in care of Elmer Eebles Feed and Fertilizer Store, Chezlee, Ont., postal code yet to be assigned
prepared piano	dusted
pluralism	see the chapter under this heading, remembering it has nothing to do with certain practices in the vicinity of Salt Lake City, Utah!
popular music	people like it
privitism	I'm not touching this with a 10-ft. pole!
rock	a large stone, but when combined with "and roll" is something quite differen, altho' equally hard to listen to sometimes (particularly through the walls of next door)
scratch music	it makes you itch
synthesizers	the sneezes of persons with a cleft palette
zipper	what one should always do up (I always like a Z word)

IMPRESSION MAKERS FOR INTERMISSION CHIT CHAT

First — a warning !

Never say "Interesting ..." (even if it is!).Unfortunately, this perfectly good word, which may well be exactly what you want to say after hearing a NEW piece of music, has become a clichéd euphemism for the following:

— couldn't stand it !

— I think it's a pile of crap

— the composer is a fraud and charlatan

— paint drying is more interesting

— all of the above

So alas, we have to let the word "interesting" die its natural death and hope it gets revived in a less cynical, more honest generation and can live again as it should, 'cause it's a lovely word.

Here are things you CAN say :

— "I've never heard anything quite like that before, and I mean that in the nicest possible way."

— "That first piece reminded me I have to get a replacement bag for my Filter Queen vacuum."

—"Most of the time I was listening to my own heartbeat — I wonder if that's what she intended?"

— "As a first attempt, it was laudable."

— "Just when I was ready to SCREAM, he'd change to a different note. It's an interesting psychological study in aural torture."

— "I think I'll come back on Thursday. Hopefully the strings will have gotten it together by then."

— Did you hear that high B-flat? Awesome, wasn't it?" (Regardless of whether you heard it or not)

— "Too much Bach in the middle of the Schoenberg! I would have preferred a bit of Schein or Scheidt and a bit of Schnitke!" (This is for quotation music !)

— "I preferred the original! (This is for quotation music and particularly certain composer(s) we've already mentioned).

— "My soul was probed. My mind was flushed and the effect of the last movement on certain of my internal organs was indescribable! Would you excuse me, please?"(This indicates you've been deeply moved but you don't have to get into details)

— "My God!" (This is for a work using religious text!)

— "Good God!" (This is for a work using religious text that's awful!)

— "Never has ear heard ..." (This is for ambiguous music)

— "Fortunately, as a graduate of M.I.T., I was able to appreciate the subtler complexities of the construction of this work, but modesty prevents me from going into details, thank you very much."

(thank you very much — with an extended chhhhh on the end of much — is a lovely polite way of saying f_ _ _ off and comes in handy when you want to get out of a tight corner)

— It was OOOOMPH, BIZARRE and BOLDNESS. What more could you ask for?

— "Honestly now, I ask you ..." (This puts the onus on the other person and gets you off the hook,)

— "It's just a pile o' crap ! (Make sure this is not said to the composer or his or her mother, as I did once and to this day Mrs. F.F. Fludde won't speak to me !)

— "Please! I need time! And a drink! Call me tomorrow! We'll discuss! Ta ta!" (This is an obvious stall, but still implies that you did stay awake throughout, and will have an opinion — just later)

— "I enjoyed that!" (Why not? It's possible!)

CHAPTER 18: THE CLOTHESPEGS OF MODERN MUSIC "WHERE TO HANG IT"

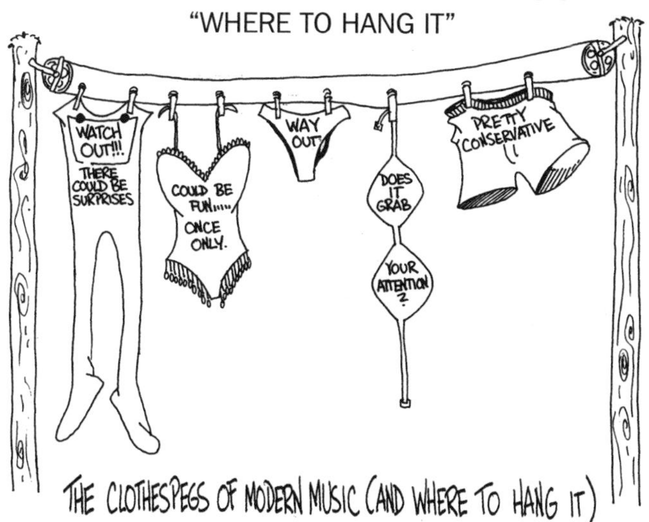

When Lucetta does a washing (which isn't quite as often as either the Maestro or I would prefer), she does, however, organize it on the line when drying, to make its post-wash-dry distribution easier.

And I feel, all of us, or certainly most of us do attempt SOME ORGANIZATION OF THE CLOTHESLINES OF OUR LIVES.

Certainly when it come to "Thee Arts" and specifically MUSIC, we do utilize some helpful clothespegs of criteria by which we "air our airs," so to speak. (Colli has just chided me for that rather bad pun but I'm leaving it in, as it makes me chuckle.)

The Clothespegs of the Music of the Past (prior to 1900) were a much simpler lot. See below:

MUSIC PRIOR TO 1900

Clothespeg No. 1 ACCESSIBILITY

Without having a PhD. in Musicology, the average person is able to listen to a Monteverdi opera, a Bach *Air on a String* (G or D usually) a Mozart piano sonata, a Beethoven symphony, and even (tho' harder) a Brahms intermezzo, and MORE OR LESS KNOW WHAT'S GOING ON AND ENJOY IT.

The combination of melody, harmony and rhythm (the three old components of music) in whatever arrangement (e.g. solo violin, piano, orchestra, etc.) is, for the most part, UNDERSTANDABLE BY THE AVERAGE LISTENER so that you can.

a) attend a concert at the Four Square Gospel Hall.

b) listen, at home to a CD, tape or record AND BASICALLY ENJOY YOURSELF

Clothespeg No. 2. HUMMABILITY

For Music before 1900, there was almost inevitably A TUNE that you would

i) say "I like that!"

ii) hum while you're waiting for the bus.

iii) sing quietly to yourself a la tub, *à la toilette*, *à la carte*, or *à la* just about anywhere.

You were able to INCORPORATE a snatch, a fragment, a theme, a motive and DO IT YOURSELF! This is an aesthetic plus. It's fun.

How often have I been caught whilst furrowing shredding, shearing and the like, recalling a favourite tune from a much-loved work, bellowing out a wordless recollection of a masterpiece.

"Laah dee da Daaah,Tum peem peem peem peem pummm,
Ta dah Ta dah Ta Dah, Tit-tle-ee pum,
Tit-tle-ee pum
Tit-tle-ee pum pum bonggg"

Clothespeg No. 3 MOVIE-WATCHING

Let's be perfectly honest here, dear reader, and admit that whether or not the music is called PROGRAM MUSIC and the composer has indicated the "PROGRAM" that he or she had in mind when they wrote the piece, WE ALL HAVE A TENDENCY TO WATCH A MOVIE IN OUR MINDS WHEN WE LISTEN TO MUSIC.

And perhaps here an illustration would be in order:

PROGRAM MUSIC

NON-PROGRAMMATIC MUSIC

Be honest, now! Admit it! Haven't you, dear reader, "WATCHED A MOVIE IN YOUR MIND" whilst listening to a symphony, a fugue, a prelude, a gavotte, or whatever, for which there was NO PROGRAM? Well, it's OK. I do it! So there's nothing wrong with it.

So what on earth do we do with the music of the 20th century? What are the clothespegs of the music of a period that has experimented, changed, thrown out, revamped, restructured SO MUCH?

Indeed, are there any CLOTHESPEGS OF MODERN MUSIC? Little hooks? Little pigeonholes? Some guides to help us form an opinion beyond the puerile

a) I Love It!

or b) I Hate It!

Good News! That mighty Titan of the Musical Arts, Maestro Colli Albani, L.C.B.O., has once again come to the forefront, entered the breach, hoisted his petards and brought to us, *gratis*, a few wonderful clothespegs so that our "smalls" won't be mixed up with our "sheets" and we can happily "flap in the breeze" of arts (specifically music) and appreciate it and find somewhere to hang it.

COLLI ALBANI's CLOTHESPEGS OF MODERN MUSIC
(or C.A.C.O.M.M. for short)

CLOTHESPEG NO. 1

DOES THE MUSIC IN ANY WAY GRAB AND HOLD YOUR ATTENTION?

Remember, dear reader, that the clothespegs of modern music have to be VERY BROAD AND GENERAL because of "all that's gone on." And this clothespeg is about as broad as you can get. As always, Colli has suggested, ever the educator, that an example would go well here. So I obey:

A. An example of LACK OF INTEREST

I don't know how many times I have determined to sit down and listen to a complete Wagnerian opera. I have sat in front of the speakers, having completed thorough ablutionary duties, placed sufficient food and drink at close hand to last through the lengthy ordeal and started up the overture to "Whatever" by Wagner and settled in for a good, long and complete listen!

The result? I have NEVER, EVER listened to a complete Wagnerian opera. Usually, halfway through the first act, (and quite unconsciously) I find myself

1. at the barber's having a haircut.
2. peeling corn husks behind the barn.
3. asleep (till long past the end).
4. "doing my feet."
5. shopping early for Christmas presents.
6. any or all of the above and more.

B. An example of INTEREST

I personally have put on a CD of a Modern Music composer and purposely and simultaneously

a) started a paint-by-number *Last Supper.*

or b) hosed down my hip waders.

or c) decided to repair the toaster, which hasn't worked since Lucetta plugged the separator into the same outlet and blew the works out of both of them.

and have been DRAWN IN BY A PIECE OF MODERN MUSIC.

You see, there are (at least) two kinds of time:

1. Chronological Time — this is just tic-toc time, which when waiting for the Chezlee Town Bus or a kettle to boil stretches out even further into chroooooonological time and can be very long indeed.

2. Aesthetic Time — this is a totally different kind of time and occurs when you're

a) absorbed in a good book.
b) watching a great film.
c) listening to an intriguing piece of music.
d) watching a high quality paint dry.
e) having an assignation that has turned out well mutually.
f) eating peanut butter, chocolate and/or ice cream.

For all the above and many more, TIME SEEMS TO STOP and you are TRANSPORTED to a DIFFERENT TEMPORAL PLANE, because for whatever reason

1. your interest has been tweaked ...
2. you're wondering what comes next ...
3. you're intrigued by what's going on ...

In short, then, the first CLOTHESPEG of the Clothesline of Modern Music is DOES IT IN ANY WAY GRAB and HOLD YOUR ATTENTION? If it does, we're off to the races!

CLOTHESPEG NO. 2

WOULD YOU, COULD YOU, HEAR IT AGAIN THE THIRD TIME?

Yes, you read correctly, inquisitive reader, I said the THIRD time. That's because there is a

GENERAL RULE RE: MODERN MUSIC:

YOU *MUST MUST MUST* LISTEN TO ANY NEW PIECE OF MUSIC TWICE

Music is a temporal art. It exists in TIME. So, when it's whizzing past you, it's hard to absorb, understand, or "get" everything, the first time you hear it.

By contrast, when you LOOK at a piece of Modern Art sitting there on the floor in the vestibule of the Chezlee Women's Institute you can

a) see the WHOLE THING ALL AT ONCE.

b) walk around it looking from every angle and direction and

c) then decide if it's pile o'crap or not.

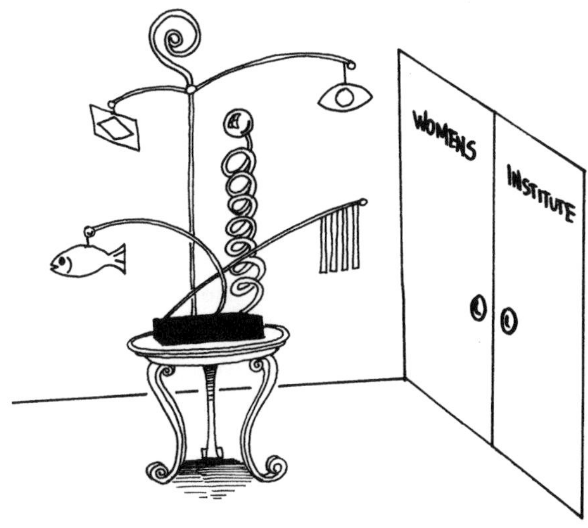

But music goes by fast, even if it's a slow second movement, so that's why, when it's SOMETHING YOU'VE NEVER HEARD BEFORE, you have to LISTEN TO IT TWICE, just to get some idea as to where you're at, what's going on and where you're going.

So, if after you've listened to the WHOLE PIECE twice, it is possible that you COULD listen to it a THIRD TIME and not completely lose your lunch, you know that you've got yourself a WINNER!

I must confess that I have applied this criterion myself and have grown to appreciate so much more Modern Music. However, I also share honestly with you, avaricious literate, that the listening chart often went like this:

1. First Listening — blah, yuk! What a piece of ...
   The most boring, stupid junk ...
   I'll never ... Please! ...
2. Second Listening — Well maybe ... hmmm ...
   I didn't hear that bit the first time ... that's nice ... you know ... it's not that bad ...
3. Third Listening — Wow! ... Intriguing ...
   My God! I forgot I had a pie in the oven ... thank you, officer, but the fire's out ... this is one of the most intriguing pieces I've ever heard even if I've burnt the pie and half the kitchen.

CLOTHESPEG NO. 3

DOES THE MUSIC ILLICIT ANY KIND OF RESPONSE EITHER INTELLECTUAL OR EMOTIONAL IN THE BROADEST SENSE? Let's look at both.

A. Intellectual: Does the music make you

a) think?

b) think about "sound" in a new way?

c) think about how the music is structured (if indeed it is)?

d) think that you'd like to be somewhere else (in this case you've probably loser)?

B. EMOTIONAL: Does the music make you

a) feel?

b) feel any kind of emotion at all?

c) stimulate any "movie in your mind," no matter how weird or offbeat?

d) feel nothing? (in which case it may be either purely intellectual and it's won in category number A: Intellectual, or it's just a piece o' crap and is a hoax perpetrated on the public ear by a charlatan who probably got an ARTS COUNCIL GRANT to do it)

But, if the music DOES cause you to RESPOND in some way or other, regardless of the specifics of "how," then there's something here that's

WORTH LISTENING TO!

And may I finally, in conclusion, reiterate what I've iterated before:

1. DO NOT BE AFRAID!
2. EXPRESS YOUR OPINION!
3. IF YOU THINK IT'S LOUSY, FOR GOD'S SAKE and the sake of ART (and MUSIC), SAY SO.

For some reason or other, in the 20th century, since the revolution created by PICASSO, STRAVINSKY and SCHOENBERG, the AVERAGE APPRECIATOR OF THE ARTS has been

a) muzzled!
b) afraid to say what they think or feel
c) puzzled
d) confused and confounded by what gets hung and what gets performed
e) thrown into aesthetic despair and taken up golf, or worse.

MUSIC (and ART) NEEDS the LEAVEN of PUBLIC OPINION in order to make the QUALITY of the LOAF OF MUSIC RISE.

So get out there, you little baking sodas of the arts, and

a) go to concerts
b) buy CDs
c) throw tomatoes if you feel so inclined
d) hug a living composer: they're people just like you
e) write letters to the arts critics (they should (most of 'em) be fired)
f) BECOME INVOLVED IN THE OLD MODERN MUSIC OF OUR CENTURY SOON TO END.

CHAPTER 19:
MUSIC FROM TOWNS OTHER THAN CHEZLEE, ONT. AND ITS INFLUENCE

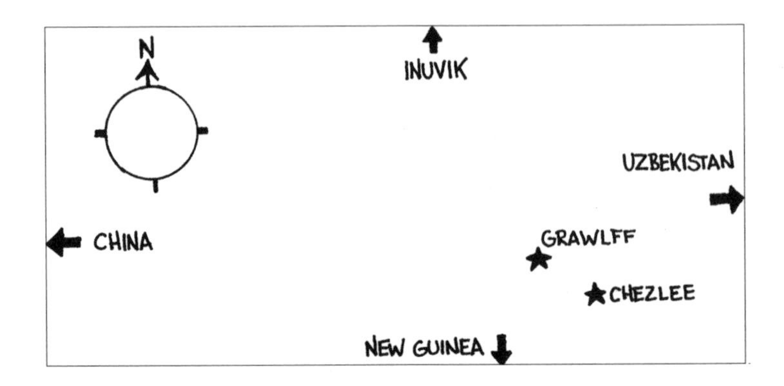

I shall never forget the first time my mentor, that Renaissance literato, took Lucetta and me up county to the neighbouring village of Grawlff for the première of one of Grawlff's most eminent composers, the Hon. Judge J.J. Juggs, county circuit judge for Sarafrax County, sometime composer and general dabbler in the arts.

The DEEP IMPACT of hearing music from a DIFFERENT AREA (they were seven miles up the road from Chezlee, Ont.) was PROFOUNDLY INFLUENTIAL in the development of my own musical style and the pieces of that post-Grawlff period reflect that influence. For example, my

1. *Inventiona Innebria* (Op.2 No. 2)
2. *Scherzo Squiffo* (Op. 2 No. 3)
3. *The Loaded Largo* (Op. 3 No's. 2 & 3)
4. *Pickled Pizzicati* (Op. 23 No. 32)

all reflect those whiffs of inspiration I got that night from Judge Juggs's compositions.

To move from this *loca specifica* to the LARGER PICTURE of musical composition in the 20th century, we are immediately OVERWHELMED by the PLETHORA of influences from music of countries ROUND THE GLOBE!

As a matter of fact, by the middle of the century, the study of the music of cultures OTHER than the great Western (and Eastern somewhat) European tradition came to be known as ethnomusicology.

ETHNOMUSICOLOGY — or the scholarly study of the music of a variety of different ethnic cultures.

Due to the fine work of all these graduated ethnomusicologists, and the advanced technology of the recording industry, it is possible to SIT IN

YOUR FAVOURITE TUB CHAIR IN YOUR OWN LIVING ROOM AND LISTEN TO

I) Balinese Temple Orchestral Ensemble
2) Music of the Court in Kyoto, Japan
c) authentic Irish wake keening
iv) Eskimo "click" singing
5) what have you
f) etc. etc. etc.

The composers of modern music in "the West" have oft been influenced by the music of these exotic and hitherto unknown cultures. Thinking that Western Music had dried up, many composers incorporated elements of these "foreign" musical styles, thirsty for new influences.

Now, as wonderful as all this is, there is definitely a down side, which I am about to reveal, and it involves a bit of a walk down history lane. Brevity being my ever-present credo, I shall select 2 (two) examples then press on to what I consider to be the DOWN SIDE of ethnomusical influences.

Example No. 1

Bach (J.S. — "old Bach") is said to have WALKED two hundred miles to Lübeck to hear the music of Buxtehude, another German organist and composer, and was greatly INFLUENCED by him and hummed Buxtehude excerpts all the way back home, I'm sure.

Example No. 2

Prof. Anthon E. Darling (I) drove (with the Maestro and Lucetta) in the old Desoto to Grawlff, to hear new works by Judge J.J. Juggs. We sang a lot on the drive home, much of it derived from the inspiration of Judge Juggs's *Tankard Toccata and Flagon Fugue* from his 100%-proof collection of *Spirits, Ales and Lager Rhythms.*

However,

THE CURRENT DOWN SIDE OF ETHNO-INFLUENCE IS WE ARE UNDER THE INFLUENCE FAR TOO MUCH!

Any and every composer can listen to the music of
Any and every culture that is practised today in
Any and every country, province, or township
Anytime!

And it is this subsequent despair that has caused many modern music composers to say:

"Last week I wrote a piece for Balinese Temple Bells in the style of Icelandic chanting with a Bedouin bagpipe and accompaniment set to two stanzas of Japanese Haiku poetry translated into Bengalese ... WHAT ON EARTH WILL I WRITE THIS WEEK????????"

Do you get my drift, dear reader? We suffer from a SURFEIT of INFLUENCES in our age so that both as a

MANUFACTURER (composer)

and CONSUMER (listener)

of music, we are frequently led to a point of despair and feel like

a) taking up cross-stitching.

b) selling everything and moving to Marmora and opening up a Petrocan servicestation.

c) just listening to Bach and no further over and over again.

d) becoming a high-roller in Vegas.

e) entering a cloistered monastery and growing zucchini and studying Thomas Merton.

f) never ever again writing or listening to a piece of Modern Music.

And it is precisely at these crucial psychological junctures that my dear mentor, that pre-eminent prodder, jabs his musicological finger right up my dilemma and says:

1. Do not despair.
2. Enter the fray.
3. Listen to this piece called XXYY#!O by the Afghan/Armenian composer GYZHCKPRR!

It'll blow your mind away.
And it did! I'm happy to say
And continues to do so.
So I, too, like him, encourage you
to do so, too, and listen to some GYZHCKPRR yourself.

POP-A-DOODLE-DOO!

When our cock crowed (or crew) this morning at 5 a.m., it really sounded like old Bertie was saying Pop-a-doodle-doo and, as soon as I heard it, I said, "That's it! That's the title for my next chapter!" — and I yelled "POP-A-DOODLE-DOO!" at the top of my voice in an expression of exultation. Unfortunately, it did not exult either the Maestro or Lucetta, who have been subsequently quite testy so I'm writing this chapter in the quiet solitude of the OLD outhouse — the one we no longer use since we got indoor plumbing. The smell is still a bit off but at least there's no attitude here.

We have already discussed the GRAND CANYON SPLIT that occurred between the COMPOSER OF SERIOUS MUSIC and THE GENERAL PUBLIC. But there is a much more massive bifurcation that happened that has deeply affected the music of our century. Let me tell you about it. It involves more SPLITS and A GROWTH. (For those of you who are medically oriented, please do not take the wrong implication here and assume that it refers to a personal and embarrassing malady from which yours truly suffers. Those hurtful hurled epithets are becoming tiresome, particularly from you, Irvin Tornquist. Attack my music, if you will, but leave my boils alone!)

In order to look at the topic of this current chapter, which, if I've been the least bit successful has entirely evaded you, we need charts, maps and historical diagrams.

Prior to 1900, Music was divided into Two Basic Categories:

POPULAR MUSIC	SERIOUS MUSIC (a.k.a. classical music)
it's always been there, listened to by ordinary folk in bars and barns, at dances and wakes,	born in courts and cathedrals for Popes, Kings, Queens & Earls and latterly by the rising middle classes.

the music of the common people enjoyed but generally not written down insignificant and considered unworthy and insignificant.

AFTER 1900 — MUSIC CHANGES

POPULAR MUSIC experienced a tremendous GROWTH e.g.:

- popular songs	- ragtime
- boogie-woogie	- jazz
- swing	- Big Band music
- rock and roll	- rock
- hard rock	- country and western
- gospel	- country gospel rock
- disco	- funk
- rap	- fusion disco funk jazz

- etc. etc.
- to name but a few

Virtually all popular music is based on the old pre-1900 method of composition, namely it's written in a recognizable key (major or minor) and is pretty well understood at first hearing and in some cases pretty quickly annoying, if played by a next-door neighbour's youth at extremely high volume and all you can hear is drums and bass, drums and bass, drums and bass!

After 1900, SERIOUS MUSIC SPLIT FOUR WAYS

1. Serious Music starting with Schoenberg, seeking ever New Ways of organizing and experimenting with musical sound, listened to primarily by groups of other serious modern music composers listening to works by other serious modern music composers, listening to ...

2. Serious Music written by composers who said "The old way isn't dead yet. We can still flog out a few new tunes using the old way with some new tricks," and this was listened to somewhat by concert goers along with a steady diet of pre-1900 music.

3. Some Serious composers started writing for radio, film or television and while the fame was less, the bucks were better so the composers were a lot happier. All sorts of people listened to their music and said "Wasn't that lovely?" but unless they stayed to the very end and watched all the credits rolling, by and large, most people did not, and do not know who the Hell wrote it.

4. A new form, based on operetta, burlesque, vaudeville and popular song, became extremely popular called The Broadway Musical or Musical Theatre. I include it under "serious" music although its "accessibility" and box-office records allow it to sit comfortably in the POPULAR MUSIC section.

With the tremendous growth of POPULAR MUSIC and the increased isolation of the NEW MUSIC composers, the average audience member has, by and large given up on serious music.

The Maestro and I encounter an astounding number of well-educated and sophisticated, well-read, intelligent and intellectual people who

1. still screw up their noses at dead old Schoenberg and a lot of other dead, modern, new, revolutionary, radical, experimental composers, to say nothing of the living ones.
2. still happily listen to re-runs of Bach and Bizet, Buxtehude and Albinoni and are CONTENT to ESCHEW the LAST 100 years of MODERN MUSIC.
3. are UNWILLING to ENTER THE FRAY and GIVE A LISTEN to the TINIEST BIT of so-called MODERN MUSIC.

But the Maestro and I beg of you,

COME BACK,

MUSIC NEEDS YOU to

LEAVEN THE LUMP.

But that's not the thrust of this chapter and I've forgotten exactly what it was ... Oh yes. I remember — POPULAR MUSIC. Which brings up another matter.

SCOFF NOT AT "POPULAR MUSIC"

While it may not be the most original and new music on the block, there's a damn big lot of it that's pretty darn good and in the appropriate context can be well appreciated.

For example, when the Maestro and I are down at the Ox & Udder, knocking back a few and discussing ALL music, we never listen to:

a) a Bach fugue
b) Schumann's *Whims*
c) Scriabin's *Prometheus* —- *The Poem of Fire*
d) Henry Cowell's *Banshee* (1925)
e) or anything of the like

However, we do love, as we sip and stimulate each other:

a) a dash of Ellington
b) a bit of Berlin
c) the Joplin rag *Solace* (a sure tear-jerker)
d) Jo Stafford singing *Autumn in New York* (slightly off key)
e) pop hits of the '30s and '40s (not '50s)
f) the Beatles
g) etc. etc. etc. till last call

— and, believe me, there is much excerpt-singing on the way home, if, indeed, we get there!

CHAPTER 20:
MODERN MUSIC AND THE ANIMAL KINGDOM

Who else but the magnanimous soul of such a Renaissance man as our illustrious Maestro Colli Albani would think of a soupcan (oops, I meant soupçon) of wisdom on the topic mentioned above? I tell you, in all honesty, dear pursuer of the arts, that NO ONE in the 20th century has ever thought to write about it and so, yet, another first for this current tome.

Stemming, *comme d'habitude* from personal experience, there are essentially two (2) points to be made here *vis-à-vis* modern music and animals and they are

1. Listening to

and 2. Participating in

and I shall discuss them in that order.

FIRSTLY: PROBLEMS AND POSSIBLE DISASTROUS RESULTS OF CERTAIN ANIMALS (ESPECIALLY HIGH-STRUNG ONES) LISTENING TO CERTAIN TYPES OF MODERN MUSIC

Following Colli's sage motto — "Start with the concrete, then abstract," I shall relate the incident that gave rise to point number one:

Chezlee, Ont.. is (and always has been) a LEARNING COMMUNITY. Seminars, discussions, lectures and workshops abound in great numbers on the vastest array of topics and music, and specifically Modern Music is no exception.

The Maestro and I had been conducting a bimonthly lecture-slash-listening series on Modern Music composers and had decided to do it alphabetically. We were in the midst of our third session — namely: Modern Music Composers whose last name begins with the letter C — when the "incident" occurred.

The Maestro had delivered a brilliant lecture on the works of Elliott Carter, Julian Carillo, John Cage, Aaron Copland and Canadian Composers (they'd been thrown together in one lump so they'd stand out and be dealt with collectively and nationally for greater impact) and we were all listening avidly to a Carter concerto that involved some electronically produced sounds. However, before pursuing my tale to its disastrous end, there are two (2) things I must explain.

1. First Thing to Explain:

A soprano can only go so high, a bass only so low — even a piccolo has an upper limit and a bass clarinet eventually bottoms out. Electronically produced sounds, however, go way beyond that which the human ear is capable of hearing, both ABOVE and BELOW. The auditory senses of animals are different from their human masters and certain ones, dogs for example, hear upper register sounds that pass you and me by, but deeply penetrate the canine ear, with a variety of results.

2. Second Thing to Explain

Betty Buttersworth always attended every session, lecture, concert, whatever that was presented by the Maestro and/or me. Her keenness to attend was unfortunately not matched by her ability to absorb or retain anything of what was going on and to compensate for this intellectual vacuity on her part, she usually brought knitting or nuts to occupy herself.

At this particular session, she had brought her pet Chihuahua, Sigismonda, in an Eaton's shopping bag with handles and fed her pistachios throughout.

Now, on with the tale:

As the Carter work progressed, the increased inclusion of electronic sounds was obvious to the homosapien members gathered there but there were also sounds beyond human perception in the upper register going on that we were unaware of. Sigismonda, the pet Chihuahua, however, alas was aware.

She began an ungodly wailing inside her Eaton's bag that indicated some torture of an extreme nature that, at first, we all attributed to an overdose of pistachios. However, subsequent events compelled us to the only conclusion that it was imperceptible sounds (to us) that were driving Sigismonda totally mad!

As the work built to a climax, Sigismonda

a) leapt out of the Eaton's bag

b) limped to the centre of the lecture hall whelping and moaning and trailing one of her hind legs

c) began running in counter-clockwise circles, round and round, using the limp rear left leg as a kind of focal point for the radius of her circulations

d) peed freely throughout.

This bizarre behaviour continued and increased in intensity and liquid volume until the Maestro took the needle off the phonograph player and Sigismonda collapsed in a puddle of her own making.

Needless to say, there were consequences:

1. Ms. Butterworth left, with her post-traumatized pet and never attended anything after again!
2. The lecture/listening series was cancelled indefinitely due to "the incident."
3. No one has seen Sigismonda since.
4. My own kidneys have started to get a little "squidgy" during higher moments in electronic musical compositions and I'm uncertain whether it is

a) certain canine-aural perceptabilities I may uniquely possess or

b) bad memory-recall! or

c) Lucetta's dandelion and dogwood tea.

Regardless, the tale has obvious axioms and implicit rules to be regarded.

Rules When Listening to Electronically Produced Musical Sounds:

1. Never take a pet to a concert.
2. Send them outside when playing a potentially dangerous tape or CD at home.
3. Avoid listening to Carter concerti if you have, or know of, a Chihuahua within a 100-metre radius.
4. Invest in Doggie Depends in case of an unplanned or unforeseen emergency.

SECONDLY: PROBLEMS RESULTING FROM ANIMAL PARTICIPATION IN A PRESENTATION OF MODERN MUSIC

Let me set the scene:

It was 6:17 p.m. of the night of the première of an opus of mine entitled *Fantasy Fanfare for Trumpet and Percussive Instruments.*

We had earlier that day collected a multiplicity of wooden and iron objects from various fields and scrap yards and assembled them on the front riser of the Four Square Gospel Hall in readiness for the evening performance. A fair amount of fluidity had been allowed for in the score for what was to be done with them and that afternoon, the boys (Will, Elmer, Herb and Vern) had done a stellar job experimenting.

Without warning, at 6:17 p.m. the oldest McNullought boy rang Obscuria. The sole trumpet player in the work, he had come down with an acute case of "summer complaint" and informed us of his total inability to perform the piece without medical assistance or ablutionary facilities that were impossible to arrange on such short notice.

We had NO trumpet player and 1 hour and 43 minutes to find one. A quick check through of a list of possible alternatives proved fruitless and the possibility of concert cancellation loomed heavily.

In the midst of our dilemma, it was Lucetta who inadvertently gave rise to the solution. Dejected by the seemingly inevitable cancellation of the concert, she pouted: "Well if there's no *Fanfare*, I'm going to the Fall Fair Circus and Midway on the baseball grounds."

Her potential desertion soon turned to elation when the Maestro suddenly boomed:

"PACHYDERMS!"

A quick trip to the fair grounds and a keg of Stoney Ripple slipped surreptitiously to the animal keeper, and we were heading back to the Four Square Gospel Hall with Tilly, an antiquitous elephant, lent to us for the premiere. The keeper had shown us that with a tweak of her tail, old Tilly would trumpet forth with a sound equal to the entire brass section of the Chezlee Arts and Parsnip Marching Band and I myself, reading my own not-simple score, would be the tweaker.

The problem occurred during the second movement when Tilly's aging synapses became crossed and the tweaking of her tail gave rise to (or rather the downfall of) several movements of her own making, which rapidly filled, not only a large area of the hall (up to Row F) but also the air. The hall soon was full of it one way or the other and the downbeat of the third movement fell to a hastily vacated auditorium. (Having been relieved, however, old Tilly let rip with some of the most titillating pachydermal trumpeting I've not heard since).

Prerequisite rules necessarily followed.

Rules Re: Animal Participation in Modern Music:

1. I wouldn't hire Tilly, if I were you.
2. Aim for more domesticated beasts who are house (and hall) trained.
3. Don't hire the McNullought boy to play trumpet due to his weakness "in that area."
4. Consider re-orchestrating for birds since their disaster potential is at least smaller in volume, although there were problems with my *Pavanne for Pigeons and Parakeets* that many have still not forgiven me for.

In general, and in summary, I would actually recommend overall that you do not involve members of the animal kingdom at all in your musical works. The humiliating ring of jeers resulting from both of the above debacles has given me a real sense of identification with

a) Galileo

b) Ellroy Frumppe

c) Schoenberg

d) somebody else who's name I can't recall

e) Una Byfould when she invented the electric tatting machine and accidentally sewed her doily to her Income Tax Return and became the laughingstock of the Federal Department of Revenue and a host of other intrepid innovators and daring experimentalists who've had to suffer the slings and arrows and tomatoes and rutabagas of public humiliation for their efforts.

Bedsprings, Sopranos and Axes: A Personal Story

Many of you (judging from the letter, the postcard and those three hangups I received following the publication of my last book) may be a tad perplexed by the enigmatic — nay, even puzzling title of this penultimate chapter. So let me hasten to clarify any queries you might have and immediately admit that this is indeed a mixed metaphor and, per usual, stems from my own personal experiences — two of them. to be precise. I strongly feel that there is no better place to write from, for it is from the scalding analysis of the particulars of one's own life, that one can make those gargantuan leaps to the general and, beyond to the universal, and still teeter to the truth.

Needless to say, it was from Colli, the Maestro Albani, that I learned this little garnet in the necklace of knowledge:

"From the hoof to the herd, Anthon, from the mole to the masses" he shouted at me, one night late at the Ox & Udder after one of our damper discussions. Anyway, if there's one thing that upsets me, it's tangential excursions from the main route of where one is going, so let us return to our titillating title:

"Bedsprings" actually is a reference pertaining to the world of the Visual Arts but it is such a relevant tale to the topic of how to listen to Modern Music, that I include it here unashamedly.

The Maestro, Lucetta and I once had the good fortune of winning a trip for three to New York City, having accurately guessed the number of leeks in Velma Varley's Victory Garden. Whilst there — in New York City, that is, not Velma Varley's Victory Garden — we visited the famed Museum of Modern Art and had no sooner pushed Lucetta (with no inconsiderable effort) through the turnstyle when she let out an extremely audible shriek and yelled, "That's my bedspring!"

Hours later, after the Maestro had been able to quell the maelstrom of mayhem — diplomat non-pareil that he is — the burley security guards did allow us to re-enter the museum and observe the aforementioned nocturnal work of art, that the curator had rehung after Lucetta tore it off the wall.

As to whether or not the Bedspring was actually Lucetta's, has never been settled although she regularly accepts accolades as to the ultimate fate of that which we had cast out onto the back 50, when it could no longer support her.

The Bedspring — as art on the wall — had been sprayed with Plaster of Paris, labelled *The Source of Life*, signed by one P.C. Minestrone, and was priced at that time at $10,000 dollars American.

This entire episode was a real eye-opener for Lucetta particularly as to "What is Art?" and "How much is Art worth?" and, I must say that her little art boutique just off the main street of Chezlee, Ont. called ABANDONATA — featuring items that formerly would have enhanced the coffers of St. Vincent de Paul — now nets her quite a financial success, particularly as she makes her own Plaster of Paris mixture from curdled whey and sheep urine.

Moving on, as ever, let us look at sopranos and axes. I refer, of course, to the historic composition by the American composer John Cage. Always wanting to keep on the very cusp of what's happening in music, the Maestro had sent away for a copy of the score of Cage's work for soprano, piano and axe called *Deconstruction #IX*. The Maestro felt that the piece would have a certain rural, or, at least, woodsy appeal and would be of some interest to the local choppers and cutters for whom the employment of an axe is a daily necessity — to say nothing of the fowl farmers. He felt that this use of an axe in an aesthetic context would entice the rural masses in hordes to the Four Square Hall for the concert performance.

Fortunately, the axe narrowly missed the Maestro's more easily accessible extremities, when applied by Miss P. Wilda Widgeon — the owner of the lovely Busendorfer Concert Grand that she had so generously donated to the Chezlee Parsnip and Arts Festival Central Committee for the première (and, unfortunately derrière) performance of the Cage work. Poor Miss P. Wilda had had no inkling of the ultimate application of the axe — namely, to the piano — by the soprano following a few ill-chosen notes by the latter accompanied by the former. Due to this memorable incident, the Maestro painfully discovered why the piece is rarely performed. Replacements costs for a Basendorfer run about $65,000 and with the hospital and legal fees it almost doubled the ante in Colli's case.

These hazards on the highway of modern art and modern music I share with you with tender vulnerability simply to indicate the intensity, excitement and, yeah, dangers that are *ipso facto* and intrinsically involved in living art today.

It's easy to hack away with a critic's pen at a sagging moment of a deceased composer's second movement, but the grim resolve in the accumulative eyes of a bunch of New York Museum of Modern Art security guards, or the fierce burning of revenge in Miss P. Wilda Widgeon's hazel greens, is enough to make any burgeoning artist consider a career change to welding or a secretarial position in a minor provincial governmental ministry. The personal price of living art is costly, dear readers, I know. The Widgeon debt will not be paid up till 2076

But we soldier on, enticed by MUSIC — that Strange Bird on a Far-Off Distant Shore that beckons us to explore ever new avenues and Lucetta is looking into manufacturing her sheep urine and curdled whey plaster and setting up international franchises and I, myself, am working on a modest piece for bagpipe and buzz-saw that has a highly moral ring to it and isn't nearly as costly as the Cage work.

Musings From the Mustard Patch

As the first rays of the rising sun filter through the firs on the bumpy knoll behind Scribbler's barn and start to do their elfin dance of light on the dew-covered leaves of the rutabagas, I lie in the mustard patch, musing on Modern Music and the State of Art today. Somehow the Maestro and I ended up here near the end of our long discussion about Modern Music and "Where the #!@* are we going?" (As a matter of fact, that's a direct quote from the Maestro as we entered the mustard patch). Quickly, however, our next intellectual pathway led us into a planetary orbit of thoughts and somehow, reeling from the giddy height of whatever we were discussing, I must have fallen asleep and find myself, as I now am, waking up in the mustard patch and musing. The Maestro is nowhere to be seen alto' there is a swath cut through the patch leading off to the peat moss bog below, but I hear no cries.

If only I were able to recapture, dear friend and reader, those staggering mental heights that the Maestro and I reached last night. As a matter of fact, I think it was in this very spot, in the mustard patch, that Colli and I summed up the very essence of

ALL ART, ALL MUSIC and ALL LIFE ITSELF (even!)

except that this morning I can't remember a thing we said except that it was massive and monumental (so is my headache, but that could be due to an allergy to mustard seed).

Regardless, I lie and muse (though not on quite such giddy heights) and feel I am listening to

THE SOUNDS OF DAWN

from a totally NEW PERSPECTIVE!

Through the tutelage of that unsurpassed genius of St. Cecilia's Pervue (the Patron Saint of Music) — namely, Colli Albani — I feel that my

a) horizons have been expanded
b) my limits freed
c) the bird, imprisoned in a cage, let loose
d) and now, I am open to

ALL SOUND! HOWEVER IT'S ORGANIZED!

And so, yet again, not wishing to re-iterate or commit a redundancy, or worse, procrastination, I shall press on, wishing you all the best, as you

LISTEN TO SOME MODERN MUSIC

before it gets too old and could, like cheese, go a bit "off" and have to be disposed of.

If I have urged, tickled or teased your musical libido enough to get you erect and heading off to your local concert hall or CD store to experience one tiny piece of it, I LIE CONTENT.

Now I think I'll just roll over here in the mustard patch as it's gotten quite hot — too hot to work ... and the sun ... over Scribble ....

About the Author

David Walden is currently an associate professor at the Theatre School of Ryerson Polytechnic University in Toronto. If you can't get to his classes, you can catch him on CBC's *Mr. Dressup* reruns as Dr. MiReDo, or as himself on Vision-TV's show *Skylight.* If you're lucky at Christmas, you can see him as Nurse Tickle in Ross Petty's pantomime production of *Robin Hood,* in which he dances with Karen Kain — believed by many to be the major reason she retired from ballet.

As well as being a cross-dressing ballerina, Walden has an ARTC in piano from the Royal Conservatory of Music and a B.A. and an M.A. in musicology from the University of Toronto. Under the frivolity and the chiffon lies the steely mind of an academic who has taught music in a multiplicity of forms and contexts for over a quarter of a century.

You've seen him on stage as Old Deuteronomy in the original Toronto production of *Cats,* as M. Threnardier in *Les Miserables* at the Royal Alexandra, and as countless counts/pig farmers in Toronto Operetta Theatre Company productions. If you're old enough, you may remember him in his critically acclaimed cabaret show *A Night at the Grand,* with CFMX Luncheon Date host Arlene Meadows. Walden has also written the music for Greg Finnegan's *Case of the Curious Cabaret* and *Hand Me Down a Star,* soon to be seen across North America and the British Isles.

About the Cartoonist

Mike Duncan is a successful non-graduate of both Sheridan College and Brock University. After a nine-year stint in commercial radio, only to rejoin radio again, he boldly decided to join the noble ranksof freelance illustration. An example for his generation, Mike Duncan has been hailed as of the nation's great underachievrs. As for his future, give him a call.

Other books by David E. Walden:

How To Stay Awake
During Anybody's Second Movement
(cartoons by Mike Duncan)

Music Theory for the Bored and Confused
(illustrations by Linda Nicholson)

Understanding the Language of Music
Book I, II & III

with Lois Birkenshaw-Fleming
The Goat with the Bright Red Socks
(illustrations by Tach Bui)

Other forthcoming books from Prof. Darling's Prolific Pen:

Albinoni to Zittersdorf and Bach Again
Professor Anthon E. Darling, B.S.'s Guide to Composers
Living and/or Dead

Thee Opera
Prof. Darling Shares His Many Opinions on this Art Form,
with Specific Reference to Special-Needs Groups such as Wagner

The Thing I've Played the Most With
A Very Personal Romp through the Pianoforte,
Prof. Darling's Favourite Instrument

The Bagpipes: Musical Instrument or Lethal Weapon?
"A controversial look at one of the world's most provocative sounds."
— *The Chezlee Sez*

Other music books from Sound And Vision:

How to Stay Awake
During Anybody's Second Movement
by David E. Walden
preface by Charlie Farquharson
cartoons by Mike Duncan
isbn 0-920151-20-5

I Wanna Be Sedated
Pop Music in the Seventies
by Phil Dellio & Scott Woods
preface by Chuck Eddy
cartoons by Dave Prothero
isbn 0-920151-16-7

Love Lives of the Great Composers
From Gesualdo to Wagner
by Basil Howitt
cover by Dave Donald
isbn 0-920151-18-3

The Composers
A Hystery of Music
by Kevin Reeves
preface by Daniel Taylor
cover by Jim Stubbington
isbn 0-920151-29-9

A Working Musician's Joke Book
by Daniel G. Theaker
preface by David Barber
cartoons by Mike Freen
cover by Jim Stubbington
isbn 0-920151-23-X

Opera Antics & Anecdotes
by Stephen Tanner
cartoons by Umberto Taccola
cover by Jim Stubbington
isbn 0-920151-32-9

Other music books from Sound And Vision:

by David W. Barber, cartoons by Dave Donald
A Musician's Dictionary
preface by Yehudi Menhuin
isbn 0-920151-21-3

Bach, Beethoven and The Boys
Music History as It Ought to Be Taught
preface by Anthony Burgess
isbn 0-920151-10-8

When the Fat Lady Sings
Opera History as It Ought to Be Taught
preface by Maureen Forrester
isbn 0-920151-11-6

If it Ain't Baroque
More Music History as It Ought to Be Taught
isbn 0-920151-15-9

Getting a Handel on Messiah
preface by Trevor Pinnock
isbn 0-920151-17-5

Tenors, Tantrums and Trills
An Opera Dictionary from Aida to Zzzz
isbn 0-920151-19-1

Tutus, Tight and Tiptoes
Ballet History as it Ought to be Taught
isbn 0-920151-30-2

by David W. Barber

Better Than It Sounds
A Dictionary of Humorous Musical Quotations
cover by Jim Stubbington
isbn 0-920151-22-1

How To Listen To Modern Music
Without Earplugs

First published in Canada by
Sound And Vision
359 Riverdale Avenue
Toronto, Canada, M4J 1A4
http://www.soundandvision.com
E-mail: musicbooks@soundandvision.com

First printing, May, 1999
1 3 5 7 9 11 13 15 - printings - 14 12 10 8 6 4 2

Canadian Cataloguing in Publication Data

Walden, David. E. 1942-
How to listen to moderm music, without earplugs
isbn 0-920151-31-0
1. Music - 20th century - Humor.
2. Music appreciation -Humor
1. Duncan, Mike, 1965- . II. Title.
ML65.W164 1999 780'.207 C99-930797-5

Jacket design by Jim Stubbington
Typset in Garamond & Franklin Gothic

Printed and bound in Canada

Note from the Publisher

If you have any comments on this book or any other books we publish or if you would like a catalogue, please write to us at

Sound And Vision
359 Riverdale Avenue,
Toronto,Canada M4J 1A4.

Or visit our website at: www.soundandvision.com. We would really like to hear from you.

We are always looking for original books to publish. If you have an idea or manuscript that is in the genre of *musical humour,* please contact us at our address. Thank you for purchasing or *borrowing* this book!